Melville's Angles of Vision

A. Carl Bredahl, Jr.

University of Florida Press

Gainesville

813. 3
B74 M
89823
Sept 1974

For Danny, Elizabeth, and Cindy

Preface

THIS STUDY was begun as a dissertation at the University of Pittsburgh under the direction of Thomas L. Philbrick. The weaknesses of *Melville's Angles of Vision* are mine; the inspiration for its existence as well as my continuing interest in American literature are the result of Professor Philbrick's dedication to scholarship and to his students.

I am also grateful to Robert L. Gale, Richard Tobias, Gordon Bigelow, and John B. Pickard for reading the manuscript in its various stages and for the invaluable criticism offered.

Especially, I want to thank my most patient critic, my wife, Susan.

Contents

1
Introduction

O N SATURDAY, December 13, 1856, Herman Melville was in Constantinople. His journal indicates that he was up early, out looking at cemeteries. He was struck not only by the number of cemeteries in the city, but also by the intricacy of the streets: "Started alone for Constantinople and after a terrible long walk, found myself back where I started. Just like getting lost in a wood. No plan to streets. Pocket-compass. Perfect labryth [labyrinth]. Narrow. Close, shut in. If one could but get *up* aloft, it would be easy to see one's way out. If you could get up into tree. Soar out of the maze. But no. No names to the streets no more than to natural allies among the groves. No numbers. No anything."[1] Much had changed in Melville's thinking and writing during the ten years preceding December 1856, but the concern with perspective, the implications of the relationship between place and vision, never ceased to fascinate him. This fascination is also one of many ideas that Melville shared with his contemporaries. Ralph Waldo Emerson states it most clearly in "Nature": "Nature is made to conspire with spirit to emancipate us. Certain mechanical changes, a small alteration in our local position, apprizes us of a dualism. We are strangely affected by seeing the shore from a moving ship, from a balloon, or through the tints of an unusual sky. The least change in our point of view gives the whole world a pictorial air. A man who seldom rides, needs only to get into a coach and traverse his own town, to turn the street into a puppet-show. The men, the women,—talking, running, bartering, fighting,—the earnest mechanic, the lounger, the beggar, the boys, the dogs, are unrealized at once, or, at least, wholly detached from all relation to the observer, and seen as ap-

1. *Journal of a Visit to Europe and the Levant: October 11, 1856–May 6, 1857*, ed. Howard C. Horsford (Princeton, 1955), p. 79.

parent, not substantial beings."[2] Emerson sees the effect of perspective as a liberating influence, freeing man to the possibility of transcending the limitations of his existence. Melville does not draw the same conclusion; to him perspective forces man to realize his limitations.

The implications of perspective, both philosophical and artistic, have long been recognized as significant in the work of such English writers as Carlyle, Hardy, and Browning.[3] During the last twenty years American critics increasingly have become interested in the subject. In the early 1950s Charles Feidelson argued in *Symbolism and American Literature* that symbolism is a characteristic American way of perceiving; Sherman Paul, in his studies of Emerson and Thoreau, also stressed the role of the perceiver. In *Emerson's Angle of Vision* Paul demonstrates the appropriateness of the transparent eyeball image in "Nature," for "the eye was Emerson's most precious endowment."[4] Using Ortega y Gasset's distinction between "proximate vision" and "distant vision," Paul examines the philosophical implications of the eye's physical properties: "Democratic vision, for him as well as for Ortega (and Whitman should be recalled throughout), was the distant vision in which synthesis and relatedness were achieved. It was the wider look in which all things were alike or equalized. In distant vision, as in Emerson's angle of vision, 'the point of view becomes the synopsis.' In the 'optical democracy' of distant vision, if 'nothing possesses a sharp profile; [if] everything is background, confused, almost formless,' still 'the duality of proximate vision is succeeded by a perfect unity of the whole visual field.' "[5]

The eye is an image that is central, of course, in the work of other Americans, as Pip's "I look, you look, he looks; we look, ye look, they look" speech in *Moby-Dick* makes clear. About the time Paul's study of Emerson appeared, critics began to recognize the role of the perceiver in Melville's works. In 1949, for example, Howard P. Vincent examined the narrative structure of Melville's classic in *The Trying-out of Moby-Dick*. Quite naturally he and later critics dealing with structure were forced to concern themselves with such elements as

2. *Selections from Ralph Waldo Emerson*, ed. Stephen E. Whicher (Boston, 1960), p. 43.
3. Browning's *Ring and the Book* and Hardy's *The Dynasts* are particularly good examples of works in which form reflects the influence of perspective.
4. Cambridge, Mass., 1952, p. 72.
5. Paul, p. 76.

the cetology chapters. It became clear that an understanding of the effects of perspective is essential for an understanding of *Moby-Dick*'s form, a form illustrating that where one stands physically or psychologically—that is, the visual or mental angle from which one views the world around him—places limits on his response to the object of his attention. The coffin, the doubloon, and the whale are the most obvious examples of objects which receive multiple interpretations. In "The Doubloon" chapter, for example, the coin (the object of attention) remains unchanged while various members of the crew of the *Pequod* respond to it from different psychological perspectives.[6] R. E. Watters in 1951 examined "The Meanings of the White Whale" and emphasized Ishmael as perceiver: "This necessity to learn and include everything in order to comprehend the essential principle is the true artistic justification of Ishmael's compiling the mass of whaling details given in *Moby-Dick*. He is attempting to see the whale not partially, as a personified malignancy, a natural peril, a challenge, or a monetary value, but omnisciently, as a possibly intelligible microcosm in a possibly intelligible cosmos. The meaning of the white whale, for Ishmael, seems to be the totality of all meanings."[7] The consequence of these studies has been to focus critical interest in *Moby-Dick* on Melville's artistic scrutiny of an object and the responses to that object rather than on the book as a polemic arguing Melville's views of life. Milton Stern expands this interest to include more than just *Moby-Dick*. In an essay published in 1958, for example, he argues that Melville's reality is a moral blank with an infinite number of possible faces and that what Melville does is to filter a constant through diverse intelligences. Therefore, "the formal problem of point of view in Melville is really a problem of philosophical theme."[8]

The artistic ramifications of Melville's use of point of view as Stern defines it were examined in the 1960s by such critics as R. H. Fogle, Warner Berthoff, Paul Brodtkorb, and Edgar Dryden. "The world of Melville is unmeasurable and mysterious. It is *one* world, but of a complex unity beyond the mind of man to fathom."[9] That

6. I am using the term "psychological perspective" in order to avoid confusion with "narrative point of view." I am referring to the individual's personal vision of the world occasioned by his unique mental, social, and cultural background.
7. *University of Toronto Quarterly* 20 (January 1951):164.
8. "Some Techniques of Melville's Perception," *PMLA* 73 (June 1958):256.
9. Fogle, *Melville's Shorter Tales* (Norman, Oklahoma, 1960), p. 3.

is the assumption upon which Fogle bases his examination of Melville's tales: "Given this world, the purpose of the tales as of all Melville's fiction is to penetrate as deeply as possible into its metaphysical, theological, moral, psychological, and social truths. . . . The form of Melville's tales is determined by the direction and quality of his thought, in which man as the seeker for knowledge is always pitted against a finally inscrutable reality, and this conflict is further complicated by the need for concealment. Since every man sees reality differently, partially, and from his own point of view, the tales are often ambiguous."[10] Fogle then focuses on the structural elements of the stories which illustrate his thesis—for example, the facts that in "The Two Temples" the narrator views activity from several elevations and that in "I and My Chimney" the chimney cannot be viewed in its entirety; both suggest that the mind of man can never fully comprehend the object being examined. The only way to attempt a total description of something is to examine its parts. The more angles from which one can approach an object, the more accurate will be his final perspective—though a perspective which reveals absolute truth remains unattainable. Berthoff's *The Example of Melville* argues that Melville's "freedom of view"—the freedom, among other things, "to become wholly absorbed in what occupied his imagination, . . . to receive impressions, to entertain and discard thoughts, to advance in understanding at his own pace and for his own materializing ends"[11]—accounts for the structural vagaries attacked by such critics as R. P. Blackmur[12] and for the characteristic relish with which Melville goes back over the incidents in "Benito Cereno" even after the solution has been revealed. "It is in this free control of narrative succession, this precise formal response to his story's advancing power of implication, that we find the central compositional tact of Melville's art."[13]

In *Ishmael's White World*, one of the most significant recent books on *Moby-Dick*, Paul Brodtkorb properly contends that the story is Ishmael's, not Melville's, and that it is with the narrator's perspective that critics must deal. If there are inconsistencies in the book, Ishmael is the one who is inconsistent. We must judge him be-

10. Fogle, pp. 4–5.
11. Princeton, 1962, p. 18.
12. "The Craft of Herman Melville," *Virginia Quarterly Review* 14 (Spring 1938):266–82.
13. Berthoff, p. 158.

fore we judge Melville. This critical response, unlike that expressed in Lawrence Thompson's *Melville's Quarrel with God*, allows the critic to shift his concern from Melville's philosophy to Melville's art. According to Brodtkorb, if what we find in nature depends upon individual perception, it is of "fundamental importance to take subjectivity into account in reading Melville; and though most Melville critics do, by and large they do so explicitly only when necessary to affirm or deny some particular point in some particular book. My attempt here is to take it into systematic account throughout one book."[14] What Brodtkorb's and Fogle's books do for an appreciation of Melville as artist is to demonstrate that the central principles of Melvillean thought, the search for truth with the constant awareness that no single answer can be final, are supported by the way in which Melville has constructed his art.

If the approach of critics like Brodtkorb is correct, then the function of perspective in works of the Melville canon would seem to offer a fruitful field of investigation. I propose to study several of these works as the products of an artist concerned with the structure of his art, an artist who sought to reflect meaning in form. I have not included for separate discussion *Omoo, Mardi,* or *Moby-Dick* although an analysis of the function of perspective in *Omoo* and *Mardi* would be extremely valuable to an understanding of Melville working with his craft, exploring perspective, but ultimately failing to achieve an organic structure because a strong narrative voice is absent. I have not included *Moby-Dick*, because I wish the discussion in each chapter to be as complete as possible, and a detailed study of the ramifications of applying my thesis to *Moby-Dick* would necessarily be so extensive as to go beyond the limitations of this monograph. The novels I deal with were selected because they permit a careful examination of works that illustrate Melville's developing awareness of the implications of perspective. Individual studies of perspective in *Moby-Dick* and *Clarel* need to be made, but for the present I wish to emphasize the significance of perspective during the decade preceding Melville's 1856 Journal entry and to suggest how his handling of perspective reflects the changes that were taking place in his thinking. After its simplest and most physical form in *Typee*, Melville increasingly became interested in the psychological implications of physical perspective.

14. New Haven and London, 1965, p. 154.

White Jacket is an excellent example of that interest. By the time he was writing *The Confidence-Man*, Melville had become aware of further implications, the power of one who could manipulate perspective. A second passage from Emerson's "Nature," a few lines beyond the one quoted above, speaks of the difference between the sensual man and the poet; this difference also distinguishes Tommo in *Typee* from Melville's master poet, the confidence man: "He [the poet] unfixes the land and the sea, makes them revolve around the axis of his primary thought, and disposes them anew. Possessed himself by a heroic passion, he uses matter as symbols of it. The sensual man conforms thoughts to things; the poet conforms things to his thoughts. The one esteems nature as rooted and fast; the other, as fluid, and impresses his being thereon."[15]

15. *Selections from Ralph Waldo Emerson*, p. 44.

2

Typee

Tommo, the central figure in Melville's first novel, *Typee*, can quite easily be seen as Emerson's sensual man. Tommo is aware only of things and relates to them as rooted and fast. Much of the difficulty that he encounters during the course of the novel is the result of his inability to realize the fluidity of the natural world and man. Tommo is a young man who feels very certain about himself and his world; his confidence stems from the fact that he relies upon what he sees. As a result, Melville's main concern in the novel is to present, in the foreground of the action, the world as viewed by Tommo; but because Tommo is narrator as well as central character, that foreground is often all the reader is given. However, Melville handles the physical background so as to continually remind the reader how deceptive is one man's vision.

The most effective chapters in the book are the opening nine. If Tommo's view is to be important, Melville must use the opening to define that view. In these chapters Melville carefully illustrates the necessity for one to develop an awareness of something other than himself, to become aware of the physical world in which he lives and the rules which govern his perception of that world. Thus, there are two interrelated concerns being developed in these nine chapters: a definition of Tommo's personality, achieved by allowing him to describe himself; and an examination of his physical environment, which is a great deal more than mere background. Melville brings these two concerns together in Tommo's confidence in his ability to escape from the *Dolly* and flee to the safety of the mountains. His confidence develops, however, from the illusion created by his initial physical position aboard the *Dolly* while still at sea.

Prior to that escape, Melville uses perspective in background scenes to illustrate the limitations of a single viewpoint. The first chapter, for example, relates two anecdotes which are amusing but

7

apparently digressive. In both instances, however, Melville establishes a world in which personal values are relative to cultural background. The anecdote of King Mowanna's queen is built around contrasting attitudes toward decorum. The French receive the king and queen because they are satisfied that the royal personages will conduct "themselves with suitable dignity."[1] When Mowanna appears, the tattooing of his face suggests goggles which in turn "suggested some ludicrous ideas." But terms such as "suitable" and "ludicrous" have meaning only in relation to their speaker. The embarrassment which follows the queen's display of her tattooed buttocks develops quite naturally when two or more individuals view the same act from two entirely different social perspectives.

In Chapter 2 Melville gives further background scenes, this time illustrating the effect of physical place on one's judgments. Once they enter the bay of Nukuheva, Tommo is confronted with a scene in which "strange outcries and passionate gesticulations" suggest that "the islanders were on the point of flying at one another's throats, whereas they were only amicably engaged in disentangling their boats" (p. 13). Later, distance leads him to mistake native swimmers for coconuts and young girls in the water for a shoal of fish. Such mistakes in judgment are, of course, very normal, but Melville presents us with this world in which perspective is as natural as gravity through a narrator who is unaware of its effect. Tommo relates the anecdote of Mowanna and his queen as something of a humorous prelude to his denunciation of a white civilization. By the end of the book, he sees that the native world too is limited, but in the opening he can only see the foolishness of civilization. He is unable to recognize the importance of his anecdote or understand the implications of his mistakes with regard to the native swimmers. We are not surprised, therefore, to see him guide his own actions without regard to the effect of perspective.

His own eager anticipation of land and of going ashore results from his having been aboard a ship for six months. The land he and his fellow sailors anxiously await as the book opens are the Marquesa Islands, in particular the island of Nukuheva. During the first two chapters, while Tommo relates his anecdotes and begins his denunciation of civilization, his ship, the *Dolly*, moves closer and closer to

1. *Typee: A Peep at Polynesian Life*, ed. Harrison Hayford, Hershel Parker, and G. Thomas Tanselle (Evanston, Illinois, 1968), p. 7. All subsequent references to *Typee* will be to this edition and will appear in the text.

its harbor in the bay of Nukuheva. As it does so, naturally distance narrows and physical perspective is altered. Melville conveys this change by continually narrowing Tommo's field of vision, moving from a general to a particular description of the island. Tommo's description begins with a broad statement of the history of the Marquesas themselves. Soon this history of the whole gives way to a statement of the geographical location of the Washington group, of which Nukuheva is one island. As the distance between the *Dolly* and Nukuheva narrows, the perspective changes and the definition becomes more physical. The geographical location is followed by a statement of the length and breadth of Nukuheva itself, its number of harbors, and the names of its tribes. Finally, because they have approached the island from the side opposite their harbor, they sail halfway around, and Tommo's description becomes a visual one.

The first two chapters, therefore, are structured almost entirely around instances of perspective and its influence upon human vision. They also present us with a narrator whose personality is characterized by self-assurance. In spite of perspective, Tommo forms conclusions based upon appearances and acts impetuously on the basis of those conclusions. As a result, he all too willingly tosses aside the civilized for the barbarian world. Were he to realize that his feelings are the result of six months at sea as well as his social background, he might not be quite so anxious to rush from one world to another.

"Having made up my mind, I proceeded to acquire all the information I could obtain relating to the island and its inhabitants, with a view of shaping my plans of escape accordingly" (p. 23). But such plans, as he will soon learn, are only based on appearance. "The beautiful aspect of the shore is heightened by deep and romantic glens, which come down to it at almost equal distances, all apparently radiating from a common centre" (pp. 23–24). Like Melville in the maze-like streets of Constantinople, Tommo feels that if he can just "get *up* aloft, it would be easy to see one's way out." Once at that "common centre" he will be able to look down and discover which valley is inhabited by Happar (good) and which by Typee (bad).

Melville's fictional account of Tommo's adventures on Nukuheva differs markedly from his own brief stay there. Perhaps none of the alterations is more significant than that dealing with the journey from the *Dolly* to the Typee Valley, and yet it is one of the alterations to receive the least attention.[2] In Chapters 6 through 9, we are presented with the first account of a Melville hero who climbs aloft, filled with confidence in himself and anticipation for what he will discover. Immediately before their escape, Tommo relates further examples of his and Toby's careful planning, which relies "upon the fruits of the island to sustain us wherever we might wander" (p. 36) and presupposes their very freedom to make plans: "In all this the leading object we had in view was to seclude ourselves from sight until the departure of the vessel; then to take our chance as to the reception the Nukuheva natives might give us; and after remaining upon the island as long as we found our stay agreeable, to leave it the first favorable opportunity that offered" (p. 33). As soon as they leave the *Dolly*, however, Tommo and Toby begin to encounter those elements not included in their plans. The heavy rainfall does prevent casual encounters with the natives, as Tommo says, but it also impedes their progress. Still, however, they remain confident: " 'Now Toby, not a word, nor a glance backward, till we stand on the summit of yonder mountain' " (p. 37). They are then confronted with a mass of steel-like reeds; this event drives Tommo into a frenzy because it is an obstacle he "had so little anticipated" (p. 38). Finally they get up aloft; they reach what seems "to be the highest land on the island" and gaze down on the bay below. What they see, in addition to a lovely bay, are natives who look like pigmies and huts that look like baby-houses—all due to perspective. They also experience "a sense of security" which is just as much the result of distance. In reality the natives are not pigmies, the huts baby-houses, or Tommo and Toby secure. They have merely exchanged the dangers associated with one physical place for those of another. "I had supposed, with Toby, that immediately on gaining the heights we should be enabled to view the large bays of Happar

2. Charles R. Anderson quotes the Reverend Titus Coan, who in 1867 followed the same path that Melville and Toby did in their own trip from Nukuheva to Typee. Coan's account indicates that there was a well-worn path between the valleys, though one that Melville probably missed, and that it is only a four-hour climb from one to the other. Anderson felt that this actuality dissipates "to some extent the dramatic atmosphere of Melville's escape and even throws some doubt on the entire fabric of *Typee*" (*Melville in the South Seas* [New York, 1939], p. 114). It should, rather, force us to examine the narrative function of these pages within the fabric of the book and ask why Melville chose to expand this adventure in the manner he did. Coan's visit does indeed lessen the dramatic atmosphere of Melville's escape, but, after all, *Typee* is not about Melville's escape.

and Typee reposing at our feet on one side, in the same way that Nukuheva lay spread out below on the other. But here we were disappointed. Instead of finding the mountain we had ascended sweeping down in the opposite direction into broad and capacious valleys, the land appeared to retain its general elevation" (p. 41). Evidently, Tommo assumes, they are not high enough. Nowhere are there any of those fruit trees upon which they "had relied with such certainty." Tommo's earlier plans are inadequate, for the island is not built as it had appeared from the sea. They have removed themselves from the captain and crew of the *Dolly*, but now they face new problems.

Tommo, however, does not draw these conclusions. He continues to operate as though the world existed as he conceived of it aboard the *Dolly*. Not able to decide whether the first beautiful valley they see is Happar or Typee, Tommo suggests that "beyond this ridge might lie a capacious and untenanted valley, abounding with all manner of delicious fruits" (p. 51). What they find, however, is that beyond one ridge lies another. Though presented with little choice in pursuing a route, they set out. "At last we gained the top of the second elevation, the loftiest of those I have described as extending in parallel lines between us and the valley we desired to reach. It commanded a view of the whole intervening distance; and, discouraged as I was by other circumstances, this prospect plunged me into the very depths of despair. Nothing but dark and fearful chasms, separated by sharp-crested and perpendicular ridges as far as the eye could reach" (p. 53). The physical realities of the island's interior simply do not allow Tommo and Toby to control the direction of their movements. Impatient, reduced to a reckless, careless state of mind, in contrast to that earlier condition in which they had confidently formulated plans aboard the *Dolly*, they can now merely respond to their surroundings. One ridge follows another until they realize that, Happar or Typee, they have no choice but to descend into the only valley they have seen. Free will, necessity, and chance are the threads woven into the fabric of a man's life, says Ishmael in *Moby-Dick*. Tommo and Toby are the first of the Melville characters to encounter fixed necessity. To realize the significance of their experience in the mountainous interior, one need only compare with their earlier expectations their current frame of mind and their act of hurling themselves bodily into the valley. The possibility of getting up aloft in order to see their way out has proved to be an illusion. Because of perspective, Tommo's vision continues to be limited regardless of a change in his physical location.

The opening nine chapters are thus significant in defining the vision of the narrator, a single consciousness which is confident of its own capabilities. That confidence develops naively from a single angle of vision in spite of the narrator's being subjected to radical changes of physical perspective. At the end of this section Tommo is left at the entrance to a wholly new world to which he must respond, and his response occupies the major section of the book. By his handling of distance and height in the background, in this early section Melville equips the reader for responding to Tommo, who continues to occupy the foreground in the coming section. Far from being a rambling series of episodes which delays the heart of the book, these chapters are crucial in establishing the novel's real concern. They establish a frame of reference within which the narrator examines and judges all that he sees in the valley of the Typees. Perspective has been of such major importance thus far that we can expect it to continue so; what the narrator soon describes is *his* experience with the savages. That the subject of the book is "the conduct of wrongly informed vision"[3] and not an anthropological study of cannibals is fully supported by the way in which these opening nine chapters are handled.

"The conduct of wrongly informed vision" develops during that section of the book dealing with the Typees, and we continue to get numerous examples of perspective in those chapters immediately following the trip across the interior of the island. Spying fruit trees in the distance, for example, Tommo and Toby hurry forward. "What a race! I hobbling over the ground like some decrepid [*sic*] wretch, and Toby leaping forward like a greyhound. He quickly cleared one of the trees on which there were two or three of the fruit, but to our chagrin they proved to be much decayed; the rinds partly opened by the birds, and their hearts half devoured" (p. 67). In similar fashion, the question as to whether the valley is Typee or Happar is soon resolved, and Tommo discovers that "Mortarkee" (good) is a relative term not to be applied to Happars if one happens to be standing in the valley of the Typees.

No longer looking in from the outside as he does while aboard the *Dolly* or looking down from the mountains, Tommo is now

3. This phrase is used in Milton Stern's *The Fine Hammered Steel of Herman Melville* (Urbana, Illinois, 1957), p. 25.

within, trying to relate what he sees to his own experience. He is the intruder, the comic figure—one who is laughed at, for example, because of his inability to eat poee-poee. His eating habits are as indecorous as was King Mowanna's queen's exposure of her buttocks. He is as helpless as were the natives of Nukuheva before the guns of the French. Such a change in physical situation should perhaps make Tommo aware of relative values, change of place, perspective. But of course it doesn't. He continues to operate upon a set of values controlled by a rather fixed concept of himself and his world, all this in spite of his adventures in the mountains. He frequently imposes his own values, those formed in one world, upon the natives of Typee: "For the life of me I could not understand why a woman should not have as much right to enter a canoe as a man. . . . It was high time the islanders should be taught a little gallantry, and I trust that the example I set them may produce beneficial effects" (p. 133). Whether in the mass of reeds, the mountains, or the valley, Tommo thrusts himself upon his surroundings, which are not always susceptible to pressure. The result is pain, physically in his leg and mentally in his anguish. Tommo continues to act as though he were or should be free to determine his movement.

Eventually, some of Tommo's judgments are modified as a result of his contact with this new world. He learns that the Typees are neither more savage nor more backward than most whites, and he frequently contrasts the two societies. Tommo also seems to realize that many of the terms used in attributing values to people or things are frequently the result only of psychological perspective. "Kory-Kory, I mean thee no harm in what I say in regard to thy outward adornings; but they were a little curious to my unaccustomed sight, and therefore I dilate upon them. But to underrate or forget thy faithful services is something I could never be guilty of, even in the giddiest moment of my life" (p. 83). He begins to speak of an "altered frame of mind" in which "every object that presented itself to my notice in the valley struck me in a new light" (p. 126). At such times Tommo experiences "an elasticity of mind" (p. 123) which is accompanied by a healing of his leg. The mysterious ailment, which is the result of a lack of harmony between Tommo and his surroundings, is in complete contrast to the healthy state of the harmonious Typees. It is only during the periods when Tommo surrenders to the beauties of the valley that the leg heals. At all other times he is dissatisfied, trying to pass from one physical state to another, and pain accompanies escape as it did the escapes to the mountains and to the valley. Almost immediately after arriving in Typee, Tommo feels "anxious to withdraw from the valley" (p. 97). As a result, his leg grows worse and Toby's head is cut open. Only when Tommo becomes receptive to his environment, and only as long as he remains so, does the leg heal.

Such elasticity of mind, however, never develops in Tommo to the extent that it does in Redburn or White Jacket. Tommo examines the Typees closely, but in spite of their lack of reserve, he learns remarkably little. Though he discovers how breadfruit is prepared, for example, the natives' mysterious taboo, their inability to communicate, and their apparently inconsistent actions keep him from understanding their thoughts or feelings. Ultimately they remain as unknown to Tommo as does the white whale to Ahab. Like Ahab, Tommo continues to trust himself, his own ability to see. In spite of his experiences, which have demonstrated the fallibility of individual vision, Tommo relies upon what his eyes see. Critics have spent a great deal of time noting the sinister implications of the native willingness to tattoo a band across the eyelids and the upper part of the face;[4] while I think these sinister overtones are all valid, I think one might also note that Tommo's fear of such tattooing is consistent with his self-reliance, his personal vision, which characterizes him from the beginning of the book. Tommo experiences much but is able only to *glimpse* the meaning of his experience.

Typee emphasizes the boundaries to both physical and psychological perspective. The views from the *Dolly*, Nukuheva, the mountains, and the Typee valley are all limited by such physical realities as land and distance. Similarly, any choice or judgment is in large part limited by location or background as is stressed on the trip across the mountains, where physical boundaries are placed on freedom of choice and movement. The Typees, too, for all their "unbounded liberty of conscience" (p. 171), have only restricted freedom in their walled valley surrounded by hostile tribes and governed by rigid taboos. The valley is not an Eden; it is a land of limited freedoms, a land of harmony that can erupt into conflict as in the last scenes. Instead of being an ideal world, the Typee valley is but one more response to life, one more perspective or frame of reference upon which man can base his judgments.

4. Milton Stern's discussion in *The Fine Hammered Steel* is particularly well done.

The narrative closes with Tommo's return to the sea, his perspective of Nukuheva no longer what it was in the beginning. During the course of the book Tommo has physically shifted his position with regard to the island several times, and his psychological perspective toward it and its inhabitants has been forced to shift accordingly. He views the island from several angles, each of which demonstrates the limitations of the former angles and itself. Ultimately, it becomes evident that a complete description of Nukuheva would be impossibly comprehensive, for it would have to include all the psychological as well as all the physical perspectives. It is enough if by the end of his experience Tommo realizes the error of forming absolute judgments of man—or islands—based upon single and, therefore, necessarily limited perspectives.

In *Typee*, Melville's handling of perspective in its simplest terms is evident. Of all his novels, *Typee* is most concerned with the influence of such physical realities as place and distance upon individual judgment. In the books to be examined now, we always have heroes who climb up mastheads or buildings, but in none of them is topography so important as it is in *Typee*. Charles Feidelson states that the "topography of *Typee* is metaphoric,"[5] but he is speaking of the fact that Tommo moves from sea to land and back to sea. I feel that the topography of the island itself is structurally significant, that the physical movement from the level of the sea up into the interior of the mountains and down into a walled valley is used by Melville as background to reflect and aid in examining the mind of his narrator. As we turn from *Typee* to *Redburn*, *White Jacket*, and *Pierre*, we discover that Melville becomes increasingly concerned with psychological perspective.

5. *Symbolism and American Literature* (Chicago, 1953), p. 165.

3

Redburn

L IKE THAT OF *Typee*, the unity of *Redburn* is achieved by focusing on a single individual's response to his environment. Wellingborough Redburn's initial angle of vision is influenced by physical and social circumstances and forced to undergo major changes during the course of the book. Some of these changes are the result of shifts in physical place; others occur when Redburn meets individuals whose psychological perspectives differ significantly from his own. He ultimately learns that single responses are subject to the inevitable limitations of physical and psychological perspective. From his small house in a Hudson River village, Redburn's psychological perspective is that of one particularly susceptible to youthful imaginings. Goodness and simplicity, the qualities which lead his elder brother to present him with a shooting jacket, seem to be characteristics of his early life. His loving family as well as his membership in the Juvenile Total Abstinence Association and the Anti-Smoking Society suggest a boy who has been sheltered from the evils of the world—membership in a temperance society poses few problems for one who is too young to drink. Similarly, his romantic obsession with ships and foreign lands results in large part from his lack of familiarity with them. Dwelling on ship advertisements in newspapers, he delights in practically every word. He pictures foreign buildings and people, "fine old lands, full of mossy cathedrals and churches, and long, narrow, crooked streets without side-walks, and lined with strange houses."[1]

Quite possibly his romantic longings are a result of the difficulties that forced his family to move from their New York home to a sheltered country village, circumstances which have caused him to

1. *Redburn: His First Voyage*, ed. Harrison Hayford, Hershel Parker, and G. Thomas Tanselle (Evanston, Illinois, 1969), p. 5. All subsequent references to *Redburn* will be to this edition and will appear in the text.

distrust the world he has known and to seek security either by withdrawing or by yearning for a different life in hope of regaining the family's lost pride. "Cold, bitter cold as December, and bleak as its blasts, seemed the world then to me; there is no misanthrope like a boy disappointed; and such was I, with the warm soul of me flogged out by adversity" (p. 10). It is fitting, therefore, that one of his fondest memories should be that of a fort at the entrance of New York harbor, for it is not only "very wonderful and romantic" (p. 35), but it is also a symbol of insular security. Within its walls he used to watch grazing cows and frisking calves, and from its turrets he could see ships returning or sailing out to sea. Such a physical position is similar to that which he has at home, secure in the comfort provided by his family. Appropriately, therefore, he is introduced in the act of receiving from his brother a warm and protective shooting jacket. When he leaves home for New York, having wrapped himself and his romantic dreams in his shooting jacket, he carries with him a gun and defends himself against the passengers aboard the steamboat, who "all looked stony-eyed and heartless." They "cast toward me their evil eyes and cold suspicious glances" (p. 12). As with Tommo's reasons for leaving the *Dolly*, the truth of such accusations is never established and, in fact, is unimportant, though his defensive attitude *is* important. He feels that he is at once threatened by and superior to the world at large. When he boards the *Highlander*, he mistakenly believes that Captain Riga is someone who will recognize his background and see that it elevates him above the other sailors.

As soon as he leaves home, however, his physical situation changes; thus the perspective from which he views the world does too. He finds that the view from New York City is unlike that from the country. People look differently at the things around them. Instead of being impressed by Redburn's background, for example, Captain Riga takes advantage of it to avoid advancing him three dollars of his rightful pay. His contact with the pawnbrokers forces him to recognize the fact that his own perspective is not entirely shared by others. Unable to sell his gun "for a fair price to chance customers" (p. 19), Redburn is pleased to find a "benevolent little old man" (p. 20) who offers to pawn it for him. But pawnbrokers do not regard money as does Tom Legare; and Redburn is not only unable to get his fair price, but also is cheated out of fifty cents during the course of the transaction.

When at last he boards a ship, an action he has dreamed of for years, he discovers that it has little resemblance to *La Reine*, the glass ship so long admired. On the first night he is lonesome and hungry in the damp, dark forecastle, "without light or fire, and nothing to lie on but the bare boards of my bunk" (p. 25). The next day the sailors begin arriving, and Redburn finds that he knows nothing about ships. The incidents that occur as the *Highlander* crosses the Atlantic reinforce this contrast between expectation and reality. Redburn's physical change from land to sea requires him to realize the folly of his earlier imaginings about life aboard ship. *La Reine* has "beautiful little glass sailors . . . with hats and shoes on . . . and curious blue jackets with a sort of ruffle round the bottom" (p. 8). The sailors of the *Highlander*, however, drink and swear and consider him a fool. The advantages of his background, which he thought sufficient to elevate him above his companions, are of no value to him; in fact, they are handicaps. Just as Tommo and Toby find that for all their civilization they are unable to eat poee-poee, Redburn finds that in spite of his artistocratic virtues, he has neglected to provide himself with proper utensils and clothing and is completely unable to understand the orders of the officers. He can communicate no more than Tommo can, for the sailors' jargon is almost a foreign language.

In *Typee*, the significance of perspective is frequently shown in incidents in which physical place is changed with regard to a single object. Such incidents also occur in *Redburn*. One night, for example, the narrator climbs the mast and views the ship from that angle. He finds that a calm sea to someone standing on deck can effect a sizable roll to one on the mast, a truth that many Melvillean heroes would do well to realize, for what appears to be a fundamental fact may often be only the result of where one is standing. Any judgment of the sea's movement must be relative to one's physical position. Similarly, in Chapter 13, during his second day out of port, Redburn remarks that he can hardly believe that he is sailing in the same ship he has been in during the night, "when every thing had been so lonely and dim; and I could hardly imagine that this was the same ocean, now so beautiful and blue, that during part of the night-watch had rolled along so black and forbidding" (p. 63). Under such changed circumstances, his new surroundings seem somewhat less terrifying. He marvels at the names sailors have for the very smallest pieces of rope and concludes what he could not have known at home standing before his glass ship: "People who have never gone to sea for the first time as sailors, can not imagine how puzzling and confounding it is. It must be like going into a barbarous country, where they speak a strange dialect, and dress in strange clothes, and live in strange houses" (p. 65). It is a new world that he has entered, one to which he must adapt. But he is still out of place just as Tommo is after leaving Nukuheva. When he is suddenly set "to clean out the chicken coops, and make up the beds of the pigs in the long-boat" (p. 66), he once again becomes defensive and self-conscious, seeing himself as a slave with "vulgar and brutal men lording it over me. . . . Yes, Yes, blow on, ye breezes, and make a speedy end to this abominable voyage!" (p. 66).

But Redburn learns to adapt in a way Tommo never does. Finding that life on board ship is not as he has expected and that the values of the shore are not those of the sea, he tries to become part of the crew. Though he is still very much influenced by his original perspective and is unable to share, for example, the indifference of the captains when a ship from Hamburg passes the *Highlander*—"To them, I suppose, the great Atlantic Ocean was a puddle" (p. 76)—he realizes that his changed surroundings demand a changed response on his part. His inadequate clothes are cut to fit, and he trades his silk handkerchief for a half-gallon iron pot. When a storm provides the sailors with another occasion for teasing him, he is no longer gullible. "I was now getting a little too wise for this foolish kind of talk" (p. 102). By the end of the voyage, the height of the mast does not terrify him, and he shows the "utmost alacrity in running aloft" (p. 114). The rolling of the ship, which contributed to his earlier fear, now "imparts a pleasant sort of vitality" (p. 115). Even the orders, initially thought to be given by brutal overlords in meaningless language, begin to make sense. He uses the sailors' vocabulary himself in describing the "great art" of steering a ship, in surveying the furniture of the quarterdeck, and in listing the talents of an able seaman.

One of the most significant changes in Redburn's basic attitude is his growing awareness of the sailors as individuals. Earlier he tends to characterize people in terms of groups. With the exception of Mr. Jones, a friend of Redburn's brother, we learn little during the early part of the book of the narrator's thoughts about specific individuals. His family, the steamboat passengers, the pawnbrokers, and the sailors are described as though they were representatives of particular classes. With Chapter 12, however, individuals begin to emerge who have psychological perspectives of their own. Jackson, "the foul lees and dregs of a man" (p. 58); the Belfast man, "a remarkably robust and good-humored young man" (p. 59); Blunt and his dream book; Larry, a reserved member of the crew with an impressive knowledge of whales; and, of course, Captain Riga are the more prominent seamen.

When secondary characters appear in *Typee*—individuals such as Toby, Kory-Kory, and Fayaway—their perspectives are not developed. The result is a consistently maintained sense of the narrator's superiority to those around him. In *Redburn*, on the other hand, the final effect of the book depends in part on the increasing emphasis placed on the perspective of individuals other than the central figure. Harry Bolton, for example, is of major significance in the later portion of the novel; so also are Jackson and Riga. As they become more important, Redburn becomes less so. In the final section of the book, that dealing with the trip home from Liverpool, Redburn is not nearly so central as he is in the first half, and by the end the reader sees him as one among many characters. This structural development reinforces a similar thematic development, for Redburn's increasing contact with and awareness of other people force him to see that his own perspective is only one of many. Such a realization on his part is, of course, in contrast to that self-conscious defensiveness with which he began and in contrast to the defensiveness which Tommo maintains.

A brief scene, therefore, like the one in which whales are sighted from the *Highlander*, is not an unnecessary intrusion, for it permits the narrator to contrast his perspective with that of Larry, the whaleman. Because of his experience, Larry can objectively discuss the kinds of whales and is not at all impressed by their appearance. Redburn is also unimpressed, but because he expects whales to be much larger. His imagination is disappointed. Though the responses are similar, they stem from entirely different perspectives. The introduction of Larry occasions that of yet another character, "Gun-Deck," because the two regard civilization from opposing perspectives. Larry has "a sentimental distaste for civilized society" (p. 100), but Gun-Deck has "seen the civilized world, and loved it; found it good, and a comfortable place to live in" (p. 101). What is particularly important is that Redburn is a member of a crew which reacts to situations from a variety of psychological perspectives; he, therefore, realizes that his is not the only way of looking at the world.

Just before the *Highlander* reaches England, two passengers are briefly introduced, one of whom is a small boy from the steerage section whose appearance provides Redburn with an opportunity to see some of the humanity of the sailors that might otherwise have gone unnoticed. Their concern is shown by the clothes they make for the boy and utensils they provide. The most significant response comes from Jackson: "I must here mention, as some relief to the impression which Jackson's character must have made upon the reader, that in several ways he at first befriended this boy; but the boy always shrunk from him; till, at last, stung by his conduct, Jackson spoke to him no more; and seemed to hate him, harmless as he was, along with all the rest of the world" (pp. 112–13). Perhaps there is a suggestion here that Jackson's general misanthropy stems also from a rebuff by the world itself. Possibly it has shrunk from him, just as it shrank from Redburn and his family when they were forced to leave New York. The young boy rejects Jackson, who responds with a hatred that is in large part defensive, a stance adopted by Redburn in the beginning. Jackson evidently has more human qualities than are readily apparent, for he would have liked to befriend the boy. It is very much as though Melville takes one part of Redburn's initial attitude and creates a character who embodies it. Jackson is not the incarnation of evil; rather this scene suggests that he is a man who responds to the judgments of the world in a human way, as does Redburn earlier. Redburn, however, comes to recognize the limited nature of such a defensive perspective.

"As I began to learn my sailor duties, and show activity in running aloft, the men, I observed, treated me with a little more consideration, though not at all relaxing a certain air of professional superiority" (p. 120). By the end of his first voyage he no longer resents that air of superiority. Instead, he takes pride in what he has accomplished and admires the talents of his companions. He has lived aboard ship and been forced to realize the limitations of his earlier perspective. The sailors are no longer viewed as glass dolls or inconsiderate barbarians, for he sees their idiosyncrasies, fears, superstitions, abilities, and pleasures.

After about thirty days at sea, Redburn comes on deck one morning to be told that Ireland is in sight. "Ireland in sight! A foreign country actually visible!" (p. 124). This is the beginning of Chap-

ter 27, a chapter which masterfully illustrates Melville's use of perspective and which presages much of what Redburn learns during
his visit to the much-dreamed-of foreign country. Having a "vague
idea" that the shore "would be something strange and wonderful,"
he peers hard at a "bluish, cloud-like spot to the northeast. Was that
Ireland? Why, there was nothing remarkable about that; nothing
startling. If *that's* the way a foreign country looks, I might as well
have staid at home" (p. 124). As they draw near the shore, he
dreams of Irish heroes and poets and "the gallant Albion, tost to
pieces on the very shore now in sight." What he sees, however, is
"a very ordinary looking" fishing boat. When he realizes that the
fisherman is a real foreigner, he decides that the man does indeed
look strange. After drawing closer, this first representative of a foreign country calmly proceeds—in the best Yankee fashion—to trick
the Americans out of fifteen fathoms of towline.

As the *Highlander* passes Wales, Redburn again begins to dream
and thinks of the Prince of Wales and the queen who rules over the
country. However, he discovers with disappointment that "the general effect of these mountains was mortifyingly like the general
effect of the Kaatskill Mountains on the Hudson River" (p. 126). A
"real live" English pilot comes on board only to begin swearing "in a
language quite familiar" (p. 126). The ship draws near the Liverpool harbor with Redburn "trying to summon up some image" (p.
126) of the city. But there is nothing marvelous about the dingy
warehouses. In fact, they bear "a most unexpected resemblance to
the ware-houses along South-street in New York" (p. 127). Larry,
however, the civilization-hating whaleman, is so used to foreign
countries that are little more than swamps and bamboo huts that he
is "accordingly astonished and delighted" (p. 128); and England
gathers great esteem in his mind. The other sailors, those who have
made several trips to Liverpool, are naturally unimpressed, for they
view the city from still another perspective. The little scene between Max and Sally, which concludes the chapter, serves nicely
to reinforce Redburn's new view of this foreign country, a country
that looks remarkably like New York and whose people speak and
act remarkably like Americans—so much so, in fact, that Max has a
wife in each port.

Finally in England, Redburn is able to view a foreign country
from the physical perspective of someone inside. The result is that
the country's imagined romantic characteristics fail to materialize.
His father's guidebook, the symbol of the way in which Redburn

looked at Liverpool earlier, is as limited by time as Redburn's perspective has been by place. The guidebook, therefore, is a symbol not only of perspective, but also of the relativity of truth. Melville's use of perspective as a structural device, in other words, does not restrict the meaning of his work to the contrast between appearance and reality, though certainly that is a part of his writings, as Tommo's expectations aboard the *Dolly* or Redburn's while at home in the country demonstrate. But Melville's central figures do not move from positions of error to those of truth. Characters such as Tommo, Redburn, and Ishmael experience growth as a continuing process. The lesson learned by Tommo and that taught by "The Doubloon" chapter in *Moby-Dick* are that the individual's single perspective, whether it be his first or his last, can never encompass all aspects of an object. The best one can do is to recognize that other perspectives exist. Conversely, the error of a Jackson, an Ahab, a Pierre, or even a Vere is to assume that a single viewpoint is correct. Redburn's experiences aboard the *Highlander* already stress the weakness of making absolute judgments: the calmness of the sea depends on where one is standing; the impression made by a foreign country depends upon the observer's background. The guidebook is part of that relative world. As a guide to the present, it is useless, for Liverpool has changed drastically in the years since the book's publication. Redburn's mistake is to assume that what was accurate once is still accurate. Even after discarding the book, however, Redburn discovers that the way he responds to the city is only one of many ways, just as his initial response as the *Highlander* approached the English harbor was only one of many.

The importance of an individual's psychological perspective is further illustrated by one of the most moving scenes in the book. To Redburn, the basic difference between Liverpool and New York is the poverty of the English city. "Every variety of want and suffering here met the eye, and every vice showed here its victims" (p. 186). Four of those victims are a mother and her three children, dying some fifteen feet below an opening in the street. After discovering them, Redburn immediately seeks help, only to find that the perspective from which he regards the situation is not shared by others.

"She desarves it," said an old hag . . . "that Betsey Jennings desarves it—was she ever married? tell me that."
Leaving Launcelott's-Hey, I turned into a more frequented

street; and soon meeting a policeman, told him of the condition of the woman and the girls.

"It's none of my business, Jack," said he. "I don't belong to
that street" (p. 181).

Even the dock police tell Redburn that he is lodging his complaint
with the wrong office. Surely the conditions are as bad as Redburn
believes them to be, but the accuracy of his description is secondary
to the variety of responses that those conditions elicit. After this
scene, one cannot help being struck by the number of individual
perspectives from which the city is seen; in addition to his
own, Redburn also indicates the perspectives of Larry, Gun-Deck,
Max, the guidebook, and about half a dozen inhabitants of the
town.

Redburn's maturity develops not from his ability to reconcile a
wide variety of perspectives but from his recognition of their existence, a recognition that carries with it the willingness to admit
that perhaps his own is limited. Harry Bolton, a boy his own age
whom Redburn meets in Liverpool, is unable to admit such a limi-
tation and serves, therefore, as a foil to the narrator. Just as Jackson
has many of the characteristics of Redburn's early misanthropy, so
does Harry Bolton have a perspective remarkably similar to the
pretentiously aristocratic side of the early Redburn. Thus Melville
seems to have created two characters from the separate halves of
Redburn's initial perspective, permitting him to show the limitations of both.[2]

Harry Bolton is similar to Redburn in both background and attitude. His home is in the country, but he has lost both parents—Redburn's mother is yet living—and has a small income. He is obviously
the son of a gentleman and also is about to go to sea for the first
time because of domestic problems. Both youths initially look for
something new and wonderful in a foreign country. Though Harry
is more accomplished and worldly than Redburn, they have equally
romantic thoughts. Harry also wishes to "gallantly cross the Atlantic
as a sailor. There was a dash of romance in it; a taking abandonment; and a scorn of fine coats, which exactly harmonized with his

2. The possibility of Jackson and Harry Bolton being aspects of a total
being is most recently discussed in Terrence G. Lish, "Melville's *Redburn*: A
Study in Dualism," *English Language Notes* 5 (December 1967):113–20.
Lish, however, views Bolton and Jackson very differently than I do.

reckless contempt, at the time, for all past conventionalities" (p. 218). Brought before Captain Riga, he, too, is "full of admiration at so urbane and gentlemanly a sea-captain" (p. 220). But Harry's weaknesses are not long in appearing. "Even in conversation, Harry was a prodigal; squandering his aristocratic narrations with a careless hand; and, perhaps, sometimes spending funds of reminiscences not his own" (p. 221). This slight suspicion of Harry's veracity is strengthened by the whirlwind trip to London, where Redburn discovers that the glitter and aristocracy of Bolton's world are largely imaginary. The magnificent spectacle that surrounds them in Aladdin's Palace is as spurious as the titles Harry gives to the men who manage the gambling house.

Whatever the truth of Harry's background, and the reader is told little, his concept of himself is not something that Harry is willing to change. He views the world from a charmingly aristocratic perspective; but, when faced with the limitations of that perspective, he responds by fleeing, the first leg of his flight being the return of the *Highlander* to America. Like the early narrator, Harry sets out full of expectations, penniless, and persecuted by the sailors. But Harry is completely unable to respond to this new world. "Perhaps his familiarity with lofty life, only the less qualified him for understanding the other extreme" (p. 253). Just as Redburn has dressed himself inappropriately for his sea duties, Harry comes on deck one morning "in a brocaded dressing-gown, embroidered slippers, and tasseled smoking-cap" (p. 253). From Harry's perspective such a wardrobe is correct for the morning watch; from the mate's it is "the most monstrous of incongruities." Redburn quickly saw his own foolishness, but Harry, "incensed at the want of polite refinement in the mates and crew, . . . in a pet and pique, only determined to provoke the more; and the storm of indignation he raised very soon overwhelmed him" (p. 254). His refusal to go into the top only cements his isolation from the crew. A landsman at sea, a man out of place, Harry experiences all the difficulties of one who suddenly finds himself in a new world, one in which his abilities mean nothing and in which he is forced either to adjust or to be destroyed. "Poor Harry was as the Hebrews. He, too, had been carried away captive, though his chief captor and foe was himself" (p. 277). When the ship finally docks, Harry is released from the sailors' oppression; but he immediately returns to his old ways and dresses in his respectable clothes in preparation for a comfortable meal. With

Redburn's help, he tries to find work in New York; when that fails, he flees once again.

Unlike Harry, Redburn is home at last, having seen more suffering than he ever could have imagined. The change in his perspective which occurs during the book is indicated in the following statement: "Oh! he who has never been afar, let him once go from home, to know what home is" (p. 300). At the end, Redburn's physical perspective, like Tommo's, is what it was in the beginning, for he is back in the country; but his psychological perspective, unlike Tommo's, is radically different. His initial concern was himself, largely because of his isolated circumstances. The experience of the book moves him physically in order to let him see a ship and a foreign country from a different angle. The result is an individual who has learned the limitations of making judgments with a single perspective as the only frame of reference—as Jackson and Bolton do. Redburn is able to reconcile his youthful idealism with his new awareness of hardship. But even that is still a single angle of vision, and Redburn's real maturity stems from his recognition of perspectives other than his own. The book begins with the narrator's concern for himself; it ends with his concern for Harry Bolton, a concern which indicates the distance Redburn has travelled.

4

White Jacket

T HE EMPHASIS upon psychological perspective as opposed to physical perspective which characterizes *Redburn* and which sharply distinguishes it from *Typee* is even more effectively treated in *White Jacket*, a book which has received little critical attention. There is so much emphasis on what Newton Arvin terms "lumpish blocks of straight exposition and description"[1] that the book seems to lack any meaningful organization. I suggest that if we focus less on the *Neversink* and more on the narrator and perspective, we discover an organization that is indeed meaningful, one which indicates how much Melville's interest in physical perspective is increasingly becoming related to and replaced by an interest in psychological perspective, an interest which lies at the heart of his next book, *Moby-Dick*.

Several critics examine White Jacket's purpose in the book, but none of them uniformly relates that purpose to the movement of the narrative. James E. Miller feels that together *Redburn* and *White Jacket* "tell one story of the world's evil—initiation into it; observation and sampling of it; meditation on and revulsion from it; and, finally, baptism in it, as the protagonist discovers and acknowledges to himself and the world his place in the imperfect brotherhood of mankind."[2] Though Miller speaks of the protagonist's isolation from others, his emphasis, like that of most critics, is on White Jacket's fall from innocence. He speaks of Jack Chase as "about as near perfection as Melville will ever portray" and compares him to a "transfigured Harry Bolton, possessing all of his admirable qualities and none of his weaknesses." Such an interpretation suggests that White Jacket's life in the top is to be associated with the values of innocence while the deck presents the world of

1. *Herman Melville* (New York, 1950), pp. 110–11.
2. *A Reader's Guide to Herman Melville* (New York, 1962), p. 54.

evil. But this polarity diminishes the importance of the fact that there is danger aloft as well as virtue and that there is humanity on the deck as well as evil. Jack Chase has many laudable qualities, but he is also rather arrogant and withdrawn. White Jacket's friendship with Jack is not "the final crumbling of the thick-walled isolation of assumed innocence," as Miller states, for that friendship serves instead to reinforce White Jacket's isolation from the rest of the crew. It is not until he becomes aware of both the ideals of the top and the realities of the deck that his isolation may be said to crumble.

Paul McCarthy, in "Symbolic Elements in *White Jacket*," suggests a more meaningful interpretation of White Jacket's fall: "The fall at sea symbolizes a fall from a preoccupation with self and facts back into a fundamental awareness of men and involvement with life."[3] But McCarthy sees White Jacket largely as an observer; to him the *Neversink* is the center of the book. Here Howard P. Vincent comes more to the point in stressing the book's title: "*White Jacket* refers both to the narrator and to his 'outlandish garment,' to neglect which completely, or extensively, in favor of the propagandistic and documentary elements in the book is to miss Melville's first and most emphatic signpost to the book's essential meaning."[4] Unfortunately, Vincent himself sometimes loses sight of this signpost and later remarks that "a simple documentary requires little structuring."[5] The concern of this chapter is to suggest that White Jacket is much more than observer. His experience, like Ishmael's, is indeed the heart of the novel.

The ostensible object of *White Jacket* is to give some idea of the interior life in a man-of-war. In order to examine that interior life, the narrator must view the ship from several physical perspectives; and though he observes predominantly from his station in the top, he is frequently involved in situations which permit him to see the *Neversink* from other angles. Furthermore, there are some five hundred men on board, a circumstance which allows the narrator to

3. *Midwest Quarterly* 7 (July 1966):323.
4. *The Tailoring of Melville's "White Jacket"* (Evanston, Illinois, 1970), p. 12. In addition to its important factual information, Vincent's book is useful in its concern with the narrator. However, such concern makes itself felt in spots within a larger focus on the *Neversink*. I think White Jacket is even more central than Vincent suggests.
5. Vincent, p. 108.

come in contact with a variety of psychological perspectives. The events of the book not only define—at least partially—the ship, but, more importantly, they force the narrator to shift his own psychological perspective as a result of the change in his physical perspective—here dramatically symbolized by his fall from the *Neversink's* mast.

White Jacket never gives the reader more than his nickname and frequently is lost from sight in the ship's activity. The opening chapter describes his jacket, not him, for he is merely the physical object the jacket surrounds.[6] Instead of emphasizing his individual characteristics, as do Redburn and Ishmael at the outset of their narratives, White Jacket calls himself "a universal absorber"[7] and speaks of the burden that his jacket is to carry about—almost as though he wished to remain anonymous. This desire for anonymity is appropriate to one who would prefer not to involve himself with the ordinary problems of the deck. He sees himself as separate from the majority of the sailors not only because he is a former whaleman now serving on a man-of-war but also because a man-of-war is a departmentalized ship in which each man has his own task. White Jacket "permanently belonged to the Starboard Watch. . . . And in this watch he was a main-top-man" (p. 9), a man who works high above the ship's decks, with therefore a physical perspective appropriate to the Melvillean hero who views life from a lofty, idealistic psychological perspective.

White Jacket himself has a theory about the relationship between the physical and the psychological because he feels that a sailor's location aboard ship limits the way he looks at the world around him. "This theory about the wondrous influence of habitual sights and sounds upon the human temper, was suggested by my experiences on board our frigate. . . . The entire ship abounded with illustrations of its truth" (pp. 46–47). For example, the "'holders,' who burrow, like rabbits in warrens, among the water-tanks, casks, and

6. The previous critical attention given to the jacket supports my position in this chapter. Many critics have discussed it as a symbol of isolation. Howard Vincent, for example, has called it "a symbol of pseudo-self-sufficiency," in "*White Jacket*: An Essay in Interpretation," *New England Quarterly* 22 (September 1949):304–15, and I see no reason to disagree with that conclusion.

7. *White Jacket: Or the World in a Man-of-War*, ed. Harrison Hayford, Hershel Parker, and G. Thomas Tanselle (Evanston, Illinois, 1970), p. 4. All subsequent references to *White Jacket* will be to this edition and will appear in the text.

cables . . . are a lazy, lumpish, torpid set" (p. 10), and a gunner's gang is cross and quarrelsome because of "their being so much among the guns" (p. 45). White Jacket's place in the top also influences—and reflects—his own disposition. "I am of a meditative humor, and at sea used often to mount aloft at night, and, seating myself on one of the upper yards, tuck my jacket about me and give loose to reflection" (p. 76). The examination and description of the *Neversink* and the men aboard her is therefore done initially from a specific perspective. From his "airy perch" he literally looks "down upon the landlopers below, sneaking about the deck, among the guns" (p. 15). His superior view is also figurative: "Who were more liberal-hearted, lofty-minded, gayer, more jocund, elastic, adventurous, given to fun and frolic, than the top-men of the fore, main, and mizzen masts? . . . The reason of their lofty-mindedness was that they were high lifted above the petty tumults, carping cares, and paltrinesses of the decks below" (p. 47). The top is reserved for lofty-minded individuals, one of whom thinks of fusing himself into the "universe of things" and becoming part of the "All" (p. 76). The narrator's job, as well as his jacket, is thus a symbol of his isolation from the rest of the crew. The reader should be wary, therefore, of the fact that White Jacket's opinions are going to be limited by his angle of vision, in spite of his declaration to the contrary: "And I feel persuaded in my inmost soul, that it is to the fact of my having been a main-top-man; and especially my particular post being on the loftiest yard of the frigate, . . . that I am now enabled to give such a free, broad, off-hand, bird's-eye, and, more than all, impartial account of our man-of-war world; . . . meting out to all—commodore and messenger-boy alike—their precise descriptions and deserts" (p. 47).

White Jacket's friends are not too different from himself. Jack Chase, Lemsford, Nord, Williams, and "my comrades of the main-top, comprised almost the only persons with whom I unreservedly consorted while on board the frigate" (p. 50). The group is select because White Jacket believes that "an indiscriminate intimacy with all hands leads to sundry annoyances and scrapes, too often ending with a dozen at the gang-way" (p. 50), a statement emphasizing both fear and arrogance, the latter perhaps masking the former. The psychological perspectives of White Jacket's friends— particularly Chase, Lemsford, and Nord—are those of men who also are separated from the ordinary seamen by their intellectual interests. Lemsford is considered a conjuror, a lunatic, and a crazy Methodist by most of the crew, but to White Jacket he is "a poet; so thoroughly inspired with the divine afflatus, that not even all the tar and tumult of a man-of-war could drive it out of him" (p. 40). Nord is a character of mystery and romance as well as something of a scholar. He is a man who seeks to preserve his dignity in an environment which subjects it to constant threat. Like White Jacket, Nord wishes to keep his acquaintances few and his duties "faithfully discharged," for he "had early resolved, so to conduct himself as never to run the risk of the scourge" (p. 51). Such actions mean, however, that he too "must be content for the most part to turn a man-hater, and socially expatriate himself" (p. 51). The man who seeks to avoid the scourge must necessarily avoid involvement in human affairs and concern for other men. Only the intellectual, the man who responds to humanity strictly from the head, can keep himself safely above ordinary dangers. In seeking to avoid problems and dangers associated with the deck, however, one lets himself become prey to the dangers of the top. To avoid involvement, man can only isolate himself.

Several crew members of the *Neversink* do not appreciate White Jacket's aloofness. Like Tommo and Redburn before him, White Jacket preaches to those around him, as he does when he advises "an old toper of a top-man about his daily dram-drinking" (p. 54). The old toper does not mind, but the crew does not always react so understandingly. His original mess-mates, for example, tell him to join another mess. "Somehow, there has never been a very cordial feeling between this mess and me; all along they had nourished a prejudice against my white jacket. They must have harbored the silly fancy that in it I gave myself airs, and wore it in order to look consequential" (p. 61). After hearing his companions' decision, White Jacket rises, tucks his jacket around him, bows, and departs. "I was shocked. Such a want of tact and delicacy! Common propriety suggested that a point-blank intimation of that nature should be conveyed in a private interview; or, still better, by note" (p. 62). Perhaps the crew's idea that he gives himself airs is just a silly fancy, but the playful and yet condescending tone in this and other passages in the opening section of the book suggests that there might be some truth in the thought. White Jacket immediately joins a mess more compatible with his own psychological perspective, one including Jack Chase and made up of "the headmost men of the gun-deck; . . . they were, one and all, fellows of large intellectual and corporeal calibre" (p. 62).

The presentation of White Jacket's initial perspective is concluded in the final chapters of this opening section, a section encompassing Chapters 1 through 19. As might be expected, his reaction to "general quarters" is one of distaste: "To a quiet, contemplative character, averse to uproar, undue exercise of his bodily members, and all kind of useless confusion, nothing can be more distressing than a proceeding in all men-of-war called '*general quarters*'" (p. 64). It is reluctance "to squander the precious breath of my precious body in a ridiculous fight of shams and pretensions" (p. 65) which suggests all the aloofness and self-concern that characterizes the narrator in the opening; the exercise is "beneath a true tar and man of valor" (p. 65).

His physical as well as his psychological perspective can best be seen in Chapter 19, for it is here that White Jacket is pictured sitting in the uppermost part of the ship, "the appropriate place . . . for symbolic self-enclosure."[8] One hundred feet above even those in the top, he is lured by the star's rays "to die and be glorified with them" (p. 76). At this point in the book White Jacket is most isolated, wrapped in his jacket and separated even from his friends. At the masthead in *Moby-Dick*, Ishmael stands so poised; and, appropriately, when each man is yielding to his limited psychological perspective, each is in danger of falling to his death. "Like lightning," White Jacket tells us, "the yard dropped under me, and instinctively I clung with both hands to the 'tie,' . . . I came to myself with a rush, and felt something like a choking hand at my throat" (p. 77). After saving himself, White Jacket *descends* to the top and never again contemplates his fusion into the "universe of things." Though he continues to view the ship from the top, it is now as a member of the crew who works there—with only lingering remnants of the god-like stance.[9] After Chapter 19 he begins to present the *Neversink* from other physical perspectives than that of the top, and he concerns himself with other psychological perspectives than those of his friends. White Jacket's threatened fall from the highest

8. Vincent, p. 75.

9. The experience of Chapter 19 is dramatized again in Chapter 21, "How They Sleep in a Man-of-War," which concludes with this sentence: "So at last I was fain to return to my old level, and moralize upon the folly, in all arbitrary governments, of striving to get either *below* or *above* those whom legislation has placed upon an equality with yourself" (p. 81).

physical point on the *Neversink* forces a recognition on his part of the limitations of the psychological perspective upon which he has previously relied. After this, the reader and narrator see more of the ship and less of White Jacket. Now begins the middle section of the novel, the documentary section. "How . . . could any writer unify seamlessly the variety of materials which we find here."[10] Surely the seams do show, but it is altogether fitting that the narrator's concern with the affairs of the ship should follow his near fall from his seclusion in the top.

With Chapter 21, we find White Jacket becoming the spokesman against naval abuses, indicating an identification of himself with the rest of the crew and a concern for their problems. And he is a shrewd spokesman, for he is now acutely aware of the effect played by perspective upon an individual's attitude, an awareness which is indicated by his assessment of the crew's reaction to the commodore's Polynesian servant. "His tastes were our abominations: ours his. Our creed he rejected: his we. We thought him a loon: he fancied us fools. Had the case been reversed; had we been Polynesians and he an American, our mutual opinion of each other would still have remained the same. A fact proving that neither was wrong, but both right" (p. 118). The thought expressed here is later put to practical advantage when White Jacket discusses flogging. Knowing that he cannot stop the practice simply by calling it wrong while the naval authorities consider it right, he shifts his argument: "But White-Jacket is ready to come down from the lofty mast-head of an eternal principle, and fight you—Commodores and Captains of the Navy—on your own quarter-deck, with your own weapons, at your own paces" (p. 147). Therefore, instead of arguing a position which might be ignored, he examines it from their perspective and points out that flogging is ineffective, unnecessary, and unlawful.

In addition to or perhaps as a result of giving voice to the seamen's complaints, White Jacket begins to take an interest in the crew. His part in the activity of the ship becomes of major importance in the passage around Cape Horn; there, White Jacket is high up on the mast, not as one seeking to fuse himself into the "universe of things" but as a sailor trying to do his job without losing his life. No longer alone and superior to those around him, he is one of "a

---

10. Vincent, p. 110.

crowd of others" (p. 107) who are in that rigging, helping to bring the ship through the storm. "*We* are homeward bound, what care the jolly crew" (p. 115) if the breezes blow as long as they blow fair?

When the *Neversink* arrives in the harbor of Rio de Janeiro, Melville uses the opportunity to introduce a number of new characters who permit us to see even further the change that has taken place in White Jacket. The figure of Bland affords White Jacket an opportunity to play with his earlier lofty stance. He describes Bland from the perspective of one in the top:

> Though we all abhorred the monster of Sin itself, yet, from our social superiority, highly rarefied education in our lofty top, and large and liberal sweep of the aggregate of things, we were in a good degree free from those useless, personal prejudices, and galling hatreds against conspicuous *sinners*—not *Sin*— which so widely prevail among men of warped understandings, and unchristian and uncharitable hearts. . . . We perceived how that evil was but good disguised, and a knave a saint in his way; how that in other planets, perhaps, what we deem wrong, may there be deemed right; even as some substances, without undergoing any mutations in themselves, utterly change their color, according to the light thrown upon them. . . . It was only our misapprehension of these things that made us take them for woeful pains instead of the most agreeable pleasures (p. 186).

This passage is not only significant for its content, which indicates that White Jacket is very much aware of the effect of perspective, but also for its language. He has already acknowledged the fact that earlier he had held himself "somewhat aloof from the mass of seamen on board the *Neversink*" (p. 174); now he chooses words— "yet, from our social superiority, highly rarefied education in our lofty top"—which seem deliberately to make fun of his former attitude.

Several other representatives of the officers and people are introduced while the *Neversink* lies at anchor. Mandeville, Frank, and Cuticle are three who regard the world in a man-of-war from perspectives different from White Jacket's. Cuticle's inhuman psychological perspective is in marked contrast to the new perspective from which White Jacket observes the world: "I sprang into the rigging, and was soon at my perch. How I hung over that main-royal-yard in a rapture! High in air, poised over that magnificent bay, a new world to my ravished eyes, I felt like the foremost of a flight of angels, new-lighted upon earth, from some star in the Milky Way" (p. 212). Though the thoughts in this passage appear similar to those expressed in Chapter 19, what is different is the fact that here White Jacket is not reaching up, seeking to fuse himself into the "All." Then, the mast had permitted him to get two hundred feet nearer the stars; now it serves to give him a better view of the bay below. Instead of contemplating in isolation some philosophical or metaphysical concept, he now enjoys the physical beauty of Rio as one of the people.[11]

Though he no longer withdraws from the life of the deck, White Jacket continues to enjoy the freedoms of the maintop. There is, however, an awareness of isolation in his description of "The Maintop at Night," for he is conscious of his separation from the life below and being "removed from the immediate presence of the officers" (p. 310). The romantic setting that marks this chapter and the next contrasts with the cruelty depicted by Tawney and Jack Chase in their stories of naval combat. "Some man-of-war's-men have confessed to me, that as a battle has raged more and more, their hearts have hardened in infernal harmony; and, like their own guns, they have fought without a thought" (p. 320). After such a description, it is fitting that White Jacket's concluding comment be no longer concerned with the "All" but with man.

What we call Fate is even, heartless, and impartial; not a fiend to kindle bigot flames, nor a philanthropist to espouse the cause of Greece. We may fret, fume, and fight; but the thing called Fate everlastingly sustains an armed neutrality.

Yet though all this be so, nevertheless, in our own hearts, we mold the whole world's hereafters; and in our own hearts we fashion our own gods. Each mortal casts his vote for whom he will to rule the worlds; I have a voice that helps to shape eternity; and my volitions stir the orbits of the furthest suns.

11. Vincent speaks of this chapter as "the most inessential chapter in the entire book" (p. 128), but that is only true if the *Neversink* is Melville's central concern. If White Jacket's development is important, then we see here a contrast with Chapter 19. Vincent implies that White Jacket is still the dreamer, "the creature of purity, who regards himself angelically" (p. 129), but I feel that there is a difference between this and his earlier stance.

In two senses, we are precisely what we worship. Ourselves
are Fate (pp. 320–21).

In this passage, one which is crucial to all of Melville's work, White
Jacket summarizes much of what he has learned since his near fall
in Chapter 19. At that time he felt that at least part of the sailor's
pleasure and purpose is to cut himself off from his world in order
to seek that quality symbolized by the stars which lure man: "We
sailors sail not in vain. We expatriate ourselves to nationalize with
the universe" (p. 76); man's action is outward and upward toward
the ideal. What White Jacket discovers during the course of the
book and what I suggest is the central theme of the book is that man
cannot isolate himself and then denounce the world's evils. The upward thrust toward the ideal is equivalent to suicide unless it is
balanced by involvement in the physical, everyday affairs common
to all men. There are powers that exist beyond this world, but they
are impartial. The man who seeks to align himself with them
achieves only isolation. In reality, Fate is the result of men acting in
response to other men. The evils of war or the inhumanity of the
naval officers cannot be laid at the feet of the gods but are instead
the responsibility of men and can be changed only by men. White
Jacket, unlike Tommo, discovers that the world is unchanging; it is
man's perspective that changes. The stars do not lure man; man
lures himself if his perspective is such that he can see nothing but
the stars. One's desire for the ideal should be tempered by his concern for man.

Having come to realize all this, White Jacket no longer retires to
his solitary place aloft. At the end of the book, his resting places
are on deck. His favorite spot is the *chains*, "the small platform outside the hull, at the base of the large shrouds leading down from
the three mast-heads to the bulwarks." "After hearing my fill
of the wild yarns of our top, here would I recline" (p. 322). Thus
both his physical and psychological perspectives have shifted
radically since Chapter 19. Chapter 79, "How Man-of-War's-Men
Die at Sea," contrasts directly with that earlier scene in the top.
Physically, it takes place below decks: "The watch on duty were
dozing on the carronade-slides, far above the sick bay; and the
watch below were fast asleep in their hammocks, on the same deck
with the invalid. Groping my way under these two hundred
sleepers, I entered the hospital" (pp. 335–36). There, "buried in the

very bowels of the ship" (p. 336), where the only sounds are the low groans of the sick, White Jacket watches his messmate Shenly die and remains sitting beside him through the night. He has moved from the highest point in the ship, where he contemplated his relationship to the universe, to a bedside below decks, where his only thoughts are for his friend who will never again answer the call "for the watch below to turn out" (p. 337). These two chapters, 19 and 79, present White Jacket's most extreme physical and psychological perspectives. His final position, of course, lies somewhere in between, but White Jacket has seen the man-of-war from both angles.

Jack Chase is White Jacket's idol in the first part of the book; significantly in the final section it would seem to be Ushant, the old sailor who is flogged for refusing to have his beard shaved. Though Jack Chase is indignant at the captain's order requiring the men to be shaven, he yields with a characteristic flourish: " 'My friend, I trust your scissors are consecrated. Let them not touch this beard if they have yet to be dipped in holy water; beards are sacred things, barber' " (p. 360). Jack is eloquent, but it is not he who now earns the respect of the crew. Jack speaks for liberty; but in capitulating to the captain's whim, he separates himself from that more venerable member of the crew who refuses to obey an unjust order. Jack surrenders to oppression; Ushant rebels and conquers. The significance of the contrast between these two men might be most clearly made by emphasizing the fact of Ushant's flogging. Earlier in the book White Jacket and Nord indicate that they want to keep themselves above the petty squabbles which so often lead to a dozen at the gangway, but the avoidance of punishment is possible only for one who refuses to get involved in the daily affairs of men. Jack Chase is a glamorous hero for such individuals. Ushant, however, is flogged but keeps his beard, the symbol of manhood to the crew: " 'Do you think, master-at-arms, that I am hurt? I will put on my own garment. I am never the worse for it, man; and 'tis no dishonor when he who would dishonor you, only dishonors himself' " (p. 366). White Jacket's respect and concern for Ushant further illustrate his own change. His list of friends is no longer limited to Lemsford, Nord, Williams, and Chase. His psychological perspective has shifted: his view of the *Neversink* is not that of an isolated, aloof individual, but that of one of the sailors, one of *the people*. This shift is symbolized dramatically in his fall from the top-mast in Chapter 92, a fall which carries him from the top of the ship to the sea below just as his psychological perspective has moved from one of aloofness to one of compassion for the world about him. Nothing *suddenly* happens to White Jacket with this fall. It is instead symbolic of a process that has been going on throughout the book. He has viewed the ship from several different physical angles and has learned of psychological perspectives other than his own. His final angle of vision must take into account all that he has seen as well as the knowledge that there are parts of the ship which he has never entered and crew members whom he has never met.

It is, therefore, an oversimplification to describe the action of *White Jacket* as a story of the protagonist's initiation and baptism into the world's evil. It is instead a story depicting the exchange of isolated arrogance for involved concern. Evil is just as much a part of the top as it is a part of the deck, for intellectual isolation and physical indulgence are both aspects of human sin.[12] White Jacket has been aboard the *Neversink* a year when the book opens and has, therefore, surely seen the evils of the deck before. His story is one of growing awareness of the danger of isolation; it is not one of an initiation into the world's evil. His fall from the mast is not a fall from innocence but rather a descent from lofty isolation towards involvement in the familiar concerns of mankind.

12. Edgar A. Dryden, in *Melville's Thematics of Form* (Baltimore, 1968), speaks of the narrator's movement in similar terms: "As his adventures aloft imply, the idealistic world of the maintop is as fictitious and more dangerous than the painted world of the deck" (p. 77). Dryden's reading of *White Jacket*, however, sees both worlds as unreal and leads to this conclusion: "In pretending to call for social reform while actually insisting that the nature of reality makes reform impossible, he is hiding his vision of whiteness under the colors of an apparently propagandistic fiction" (p. 78).

5

Pierre

THE THEMATIC and structural differences in Melville's works before and after 1851 have been a topic of frequent critical concern. The change in narrative technique marked by the shift from a first- to a third-person narrator and by a diminution in the scale of the subject matter are often noted, as is the sense, in the later writings, of futility, bitterness, and fatality. This shift is mirrored in the handling of perspective. Though it remains of central importance, perspective is not always handled as it was before *Moby-Dick.* Its use in *Typee, Redburn,* and *White Jacket* emphasizes the danger of mistaking the isolated perspective for comprehensive truth. Redburn and White Jacket, in particular, move from positions of isolation to ones from which they recognize the limitations effected by perspective. The darkness of a book like *Pierre* is very much the result of having a central figure who also exchanges his early isolation but for even greater subsequent isolation. Significantly, that movement is accompanied by a physical exchange of the outdoors for the indoors and of the ground levels for the upper floors, just the opposite of the movement we have noted in *Redburn* and *White Jacket.*

The opening chapters of *Pierre* present the central figure in a world characterized by comfort, beauty, health, and repose. Pierre is first seen on a morning that would make a sojourner from the city "wonder-smitten with the trance-like aspect of the green and golden world."[1] "Dewily refreshed and spiritualized by sleep, . . . half unconsciously" (p. 1), he bends his steps towards Lucy's cottage, where he lifts his eyes to gaze upon her upper window. Both of these actions, walking outdoors and gazing upwards, are character-

1. *Pierre: Or, the Ambiguities,* ed. Henry A. Murray (New York, 1949), p. 1. All subsequent references to *Pierre* will be to this edition and will appear in the text.

39

istic of the early Pierre. It was his "choice fate to have been born
and nurtured in the country" (p. 4). His visits to the city have been
limited to annual ones and then only in the company of his parents.
Pierre enjoys both the poetical qualities of the country, reflected in
the way he and his mother act and speak towards each other, and
the physical qualities. He loves the outdoors, and "generally rose
with the sun, and could not sleep without riding his twenty, or
walking his twelve miles a day, or felling a fair-sized hemlock in the
forest, or boxing, or fencing, or boating, or performing some other
gymnastical feat" (p. 17). Pierre idolizes—and knows only—beauty
and health. He stands upon a "noble pedestal" (p. 11) from which
he gazes in rapture at his background, his sweetheart Lucy, and his
mother. Each is in turn pedestaled and reverenced by the romantic
Pierre.

Pierre is a boy of "absolute motives" (p. 5). If his story had been
written five years earlier, Melville might have had his hero eventually realize the limitations of such absolutes; as it stands, however,
when Pierre learns that these particular absolutes are wrong, he
rapidly adopts others. In the beginning he believes that his past life,
his mother, his father, Lucy, and Saddle Meadows all are perfect.
Even his daydreams are expressed in absolute terms: " 'Oh, had
my father but had a daughter! . . . Someone whom I might love,
and protect, and fight for, if need be. It must be a glorious thing
to engage in a mortal quarrel on a sweet sister's behalf' " (p. 6).
Physically Pierre exists in a dewy, timeless, outdoors world; psychologically he sees objects surrounding him as perfections, as absolutes. The physical and the psychological are further brought together in this opening section when Pierre and Lucy go for a picnic
into the hills. But the picnic ends in tears, for Lucy is overcome by
sadness. Instead of being exhilarated as is Pierre, she thinks of the
mysterious face which haunts him and about which he has told her.
Both lovers are seized by a foretaste of the future with the realization that their happiness may be destroyed. " 'Up, my Pierre; let
us up, and fly these hills, whence, I fear, too wide a prospect meets
us' " (p. 44). Just as the hills offer a new and sweeping physical
perspective of the countryside, so are the lovers now forced to realize that perhaps the way in which they previously have viewed
their love and future is too limited. "Now they rolled swiftly down
the slopes; nor tempted the upper hills; but sped fast for the plain.
Now the cloud hath passed from Lucy's eye; no more the lurid

slanting light forks upward from her lover's brow. In the plain they find peace, and love, and joy again" (p. 44). But such joy has been shown to be the result of a limited view of the world. Pierre's parting words to Lucy after the picnic, " 'The great God wrap thee ever, Lucy' " are certainly appropriate, for in the hills they have sensed that their happiness will be threatened when their world and their perspective of that world are no longer wrapped in seclusion.

Pierre never looks at the world in other than absolute terms. In the beginning he is aware only of absolute perfection and joy; at the end he seeks only absolute Truth. He never reconciles the various angles of vision by realizing that man cannot hope to comprehend absolutes. When his early world begins to crack and his youthful thoughts of his father and mother are shattered, he seeks new ideals. Pondering the haunting face of Isabel, he warns the gods to beware destroying his faith, for he will be forced to another extreme.

"It visibly rustles behind the concealing screen. Now, never into the soul of Pierre, stole there before, a muffledness like this! If aught really lurks in it, ye sovereign powers that claim all my leal worshipings, I conjure ye to lift the veil; . . . advance I on a precipice, hold me back; but abandon me to an unknown misery, that it shall suddenly seize me, and possess me, wholly,—that ye will never do; else, Pierre's fond faith in ye—now clean, untouched—may clean depart; and give me up to be a railing atheist" (pp. 47–48).

His world of "visible, beautiful flesh, and audible breath" (p. 56) is suddenly entered and destroyed by the appearance of Isabel, a dark-haired girl who claims to be his sister. Unquestioning, he believes her and acts upon that belief: "He equivocated with himself no more; the gloom of the air had now burst into his heart, and extinguished its light; then, first in all his life, Pierre felt the irresistible admonitions and intuitions of Fate" (p. 72). In this and many similar statements throughout the book, the narrator, and Pierre himself, descry the intervention of Fate. The actions of the characters, however, are frequently the result of the way in which they themselves respond to their world. Unlike Redburn, White Jacket, and Ishmael—all of whom become aware of a wide variety of perspectives—Ahab and Pierre embrace one perspective at the expense of all others. When Pierre discovers the limitations of his youthful world, he rejects that world utterly and devotes himself fully to a new one, never recognizing that it too is equally limited. The world of Saddle Meadows is one of sensuous beauty, in which Pierre immerses himself. After the intrusion of less pleasant truths about human existence, truths which balance rather than supersede the beauties of life, Pierre shifts his focus and immerses himself in the quest for absolute Truth. Initially an enthusiast, he dies an enthusiast. He does little more than shift the direction of his enthusiasm. Once that change has occurred, Pierre's psychological perspective becomes increasingly narrowed as his view of the world becomes more limited. Though he dedicates himself to Truth, he recognizes only one of its many aspects. Gradually, like Ahab, his concept of himself as one driven by Fate results in an introverted angle of vision which sees little else but its own narrow world.

Although his first act after reading Isabel's letter is to rush wildly out of doors, his tendency during the remainder of the book is to withdraw gradually into enclosed areas. The book begins in the lush morning air and ends in a stark jail cell. His increasingly limited psychological perspective is thus paralleled by an equally limited physical perspective. After dashing outside, he returns home and enters "a locked, round-windowed closet connecting" with his bedroom, where he keeps a portrait of his father and where "he had always been wont to go, in those sweetly awful hours, when the spirit crieth to the spirit, Come into solitude with me, twin-brother" (p. 83). The portrait is one of two in the house, the same man viewed from two distinct perspectives. The picture in Pierre's closet is that of "a brisk, unentangled, young bachelor"; the larger of the two, that hanging in the family drawing-room, portrays "a middle-aged, married man" and is a portrait indicating all the respectable qualities appropriate to the wedded state. So distinct are the paintings that Mrs. Glendinning cannot stand Pierre's because it presents a view of her husband that she does not want to accept. The warning of the closet portrait is to "believe not the drawing-room painting; that is not thy father; or, at least, is not *all* of thy father. Consider in thy mind, Pierre, whether we two paintings may not make only one" (p. 97). After Isabel's letter, however, Pierre accepts only the closet painting. His father's shrine, before which he used to worship, lies in rubble at his feet. He fails to see that if the drawing-room painting before was not all of his father, now neither is the closet painting all. Each is a perspective of limited validity, and each should be recognized as such. But the father's memory, which was once sacred to Pierre, is now anathema.

"Now, from his height of composure, he firmly gazed abroad upon the charred landscape within him" (p. 101). From this new psychological perspective, appropriately expressed in physical terms, Pierre chooses to act, but he is less concerned with what he must do than with how he must do it. In this first aftermath of the receipt of Isabel's letter, Pierre is confident that he knows how everyone involved will respond to Isabel. "Wonderful, indeed, was the electric insight which Fate had now given him into the vital character of his mother. She well might have stood all ordinary tests; but when Pierre thought of the touchstone of his immense strait applied to her spirit; he felt profoundly assured that she would crumble into nothing before it" (p. 104). Whether or not this assumption is true, Pierre acts as though it were and is thus an example of White Jacket's statement that "Ourselves are Fate." He anticipates the thoughts of others as well as their actions and determines his own course accordingly. If Fate is responsible for Isabel's appearance, Pierre must at least share responsibility for the events which follow.

"Standing helf-befogged upon the mountain of his Fate" (p. 123) —another psychological state expressed in physical terms—Pierre decides to embrace Isabel at the expense of his mother, Lucy, and Saddle Meadows. That embrace, in its physical sense, is frequently described in such a way as to show the limited view that Pierre has of the whole situation. As he embraces Isabel, he feels "a faint struggling within his clasp; her head drooped against him; his whole form was bathed in the flowing glossiness of her long and unimprisoned hair" (p. 132). Though Pierre associates Isabel with the Absolute, she is described in terms which suggest confinement. Her first memories, for example, are of houses, and she is seldom seen out of doors. Whether enveloped by her hair, lying beneath the Memnon Stone, or locked within his closet, Pierre is no longer the healthy, robust youth who loved exercise and nature: " 'But truly, Isabel, thy all-abounding hair falls upon me with some spell which dismisses all ordinary considerations from me' " (p. 170).

Pierre's psychological perspective at this time continues to be presented in physical terms. "Sudden onsets of new truth will assail him, and overturn him as the Tartars did China; for there is no China Wall that man can build in his soul, which shall permanently stay the irruptions of those barbarous hordes which Truth ever nourishes in the loins of her frozen, yet teeming North" (p. 196). He attempts to build such a China Wall and, like Tommo as he plans a course of action based upon his shipboard view of Nukuheva, relies entirely upon the way things appear to him. As also in *Typee*, Melville therefore uses vision as a basic image. Whether or not, for example, it is a blessing that intricacies "are mostly withheld from sight" when man is about to make a decision depends entirely upon "what view you take of it" (p. 206). In such an individual's "eagerness, all objects are deceptively foreshortened; by his intensity each object is viewed as detached; so that essentially and relatively everything is misseen by him" (p. 206), and he thus may be fittingly described as a "blind mole" (p. 207). Pierre's decision to present Isabel to the world as his wife is the result of two absolute convictions: he must give lasting fraternal help to Isabel and he must make sure that the world keeps his father's memory untouched. Therefore casting off his former way of looking at the world of Saddle Meadows, as well as all physical ties to it, Pierre sets off for New York in the company of Isabel and her friend Delly Ulver.

The transition of the three from Saddle Meadows to their New York home at the Apostles' is punctuated by the importance of perspective. Objects which once appeared one way now appear another. The mementoes which Pierre sorts out before he leaves are seen as the remnants of the "decay and death of endless innumerable generations" (p. 232). The pamphlet on chronometricals and horologicals is a different psychological perspective on Pierre's dilemma, presenting a philosophy as extreme and, therefore, as fallacious and unacceptable as is Pierre's itself. Yet Pierre's salvation might lie in recognizing this other viewpoint, in seeing its relativism as a qualification of and ironic commentary upon his own absolutism. For the time, however, he forgets and "loses" the pamphlet. We are told that he is unable to comprehend its "central conceit," but perhaps his handling of the pamphlet symbolizes a suppressing of the complexities and alternatives suggested in it. Finally, Pierre's relationship with Glen Stanly is itself an extended example of perspective. The love-friendship that seems absolute to boys looks very different when they grow older: "The mere outer friendship may in some degree—greater or less—survive; but the singular love in it has perishingly dropped away" (p. 255). Part of the change is attributed by the narrator to change of place as well as change of age: "If the general love for women had in Pierre sensibly modified his particular sentiment toward Glen; neither had the thousand nameless fascinations of the then brilliant paradises of France and Italy, failed to exert their seductive influence on many of the previous feelings of Glen" (p. 256). No effort of will is able to retrieve that former friendship once the psychological perspective has shifted, but both perspectives—then and now—are equally valid.

After settling his dependents at the Apostles', Pierre decides to support his household by writing. But even the art of writing is seen in a new light. Popular writing results only in fame, and Pierre now sees himself as a seeker of Truth. Appropriate to this lofty attitude is Pierre's room at the Apostles'. It is at the rear and near the top of the building, and from it he gazes down on a "wilderness of tiles, slate, shingles, and tin" (p. 318) and a gray tower, "emblem to Pierre of an unshakable fortitude" (p. 318). Physically isolated from the world, Pierre works but discovers only the impossibility of knowing Truth, an impossibility described by the narrator in terms similar to those used to describe Tommo's journey into the mountains of Nukuheva. "But, as to the resolute traveler in Switzerland, the Alps do never in one wide and comprehensive sweep, instantaneously reveal their full awfulness of amplitude; . . . so hath heaven wisely ordained, that on first entering into the Switzerland of his soul, man shall not at once perceive its tremendous immensity" (p. 334). Such an image suggests, as the narrator himself is aware, that the mountain can be climbed. But "far over the invisible Atlantic, the Rocky Mountains and the Andes are yet unbeheld" (p. 335). Man can climb but one mountain at a time; he can never see more than single aspects of Truth. As Pierre gradually realizes his human limitations, his work slowly comes to a halt. Like his physical movement from the warm, country outdoors to a cold, lofty room in the city, his psychological movement has also been in the direction of cold, lofty absolutes. When he becomes aware that other mountains loom beyond each one he climbs, he understands that he can live neither as an ordinary man nor as a seeker for Truth. He is unwilling to accept without challenge the limitations of the human condition, and yet those same limitations keep him from ever fully comprehending Truth. "For Faith and philosophy are air, but events are brass. Amidst his gray philosophizings, Life breaks upon a man like a morning" (p. 340).

Willingly having deserted humanity and suddenly discovering himself deserted by the gods, Pierre becomes completely unable to act. In the final chapters the action which most characterizes him is that of sitting: "And now day succeeds day, and week follows week, and Pierre still sits in his chamber" (p. 347), missing the life that goes on in the city around him. He is finally joined in that isolation by Lucy, called, she feels, by God as was Pierre earlier: "She had been moved to it by all-encompassing influences above, around, and beneath" (p. 384), moved to enter a cold upper room where she can sit by Pierre in his "sublime heaven of heroism" (p. 365). Lofty sentiments such as these are often reinforced by other phrases repeated in an almost hypnotic manner. In Book 19, for example, "on the third night following the arrival of the party in the city, Pierre sat at twilight by a lofty window in the rear building of the Apostles'" (p. 317) is repeated three times in four paragraphs with only slight variation in word order. The effect of such passages, like the emphasis placed upon physical location and the magical guitar, is to stress the isolated, unworldly psychological perspective of Pierre. Pierre has withdrawn into a world all his own—"'I render no accounts: I am what I am'" (p. 382)—but it is impossible to exist under such limited conditions, for both physically and intellectually Pierre feeds upon himself. Death is inevitable.

Unlike the heroes discussed before—Redburn, White Jacket, even Tommo—Pierre never learns that one's response to his world is frequently the result not of the world's condition but of the way in which one perceives that condition. Redburn and White Jacket move from positions of isolation towards ones in which they communicate. Misanthropy and distrust are exchanged for interest and concern. Pierre, however, feels that life has "taught him never to expect any good from any thing; but always to anticipate ill" (p. 389). As a result, though "in a city of hundreds of thousands of human beings, Pierre was solitary as at the Pole" (p. 398). When the beautiful existence at Saddle Meadows is shattered by Isabel's letter, he seeks a different ideal, never realizing that both ideals might have some relation to each other. When his search proves fruitless and he sees the "everlasting elusiveness of Truth" (p. 399), he is unable to respond in any way but with despair and is content only in his closed room or obscure dark alleys. Appropriately, for one who is blind to any psychological perspective but his own, Pierre's eyes begin to fail; he is no longer able even to write.

Just before his death, Pierre dreams of the Mount of Titans, which stands alone some fifteen miles from his home at Saddle Meadows. "The height, viewed from the piazza of a soft haze-canopied summer's noon, presented a long and beautiful, but not entirely inaccessible-looking purple precipice, some two thousand feet in air, and on each hand sideways sloping down to lofty terraces of pastures" (p. 403). White flowers cover the pastures. Though beautiful to the eye, these same flowers are distasteful to cattle and thus are harmful to farmers on the hillsides. Differences occur as one's physical perspective changes and he approaches the mountain: "Coming still more nigh, long and frequent rents among the mass of leaves revealed horrible glimpses of dark-dripping rocks, and mysterious mouths of wolfish caves" (p. 403). Just as Pierre leaves his home to seek Truth, an endeavor resulting in frustration and failure, so may one set out to visit the beautiful mountain. The end of the journey, however, results in anything but the realization of beauty. "Stark desolation; ruin, merciless and ceaseless; chills and gloom,—all here lived a hidden life, curtained by that cunning purpleness, which, from the piazza of the manor-house, so beautifully invested the mountain once called Delectable, but now styled Titanic" (p. 405).

Finally, having "sat on earth's saddle" until he is weary and, like his grandfather, unhorsed, Pierre commits suicide, symbolically if not also literally, by killing his cousin. "Spatterings of his own kindred blood were upon the pavement; his own hand had extinguished his house in slaughtering the only unoutlawed human being by the name of Glendinning;—and Pierre was seized by a hundred contending hands" (p. 424). The narrator talks a great deal about Fate, suggesting that his hero is the puppet of outside forces, a possibility which would mean that Pierre's death is less a suicide than a homicide. However, in addition to presenting all the circumstances of the situation, the narrator also emphasizes that Pierre's course of action is the result of his own choices. It is his choice that brings Isabel, Delly, and himself to New York. To cry "Fate" is to refuse to see the relationship between perspective and responsibility. Perspective influences, it does not determine. The individual's awareness of or refusal to see its effect contributes to his psychological perspective. Tommo, Redburn, White Jacket, and Ishmael initially yield to their physical perspectives, thereby inviting destruction; however, the fact that each can finally act on some other basis than physical perspective suggests that will is a major ingredient in psychological perspective and, therefore, in action. Redburn, for example, learns that his perspective is only one of many and is able to act on that knowledge. Neither his early misanthropy nor his later concern for others is determined totally by circumstances. He, too, is responsible for his psychological perspective and for the action that results. What is fated, given the indifferent Melvillean universe (one which functions solely on the principles of cause and effect) is not action but the consequences of that action. Tommo's venture into the mountains or White Jacket's ascent to the masthead, actions which they are free to initiate, indicate that the only result of such movement can be failure and self-destruction. If powers beyond man's understanding exist, they are characterized as impassive. Only the proud ego of an Ahab or a Pierre is able to imagine itself significant to the gods.

6

Israel Potter
and
The Confidence-Man

THE LAST major works of fiction in this first decade of Melville's writing present an even greater change in the handling of perspective than the changes already discussed. At the same time, the ideas expressed in *Israel Potter* and *The Confidence-Man* are also very different from anything Melville has worked with before. The possibilities for individual achievement and personal growth, for example—possibilities which are realized in characters like White Jacket and Ishmael—are missing in these final two works. Absent also is the function of psychological perspective as the reflection of a character's awareness of himself within his physical environment. Considering how well delineated is the individual's psychological perspective in works prior to *Israel Potter*, the reader is scarcely prepared to meet the faceless heroes of these last books. There is clearly a fundamental difference in fictional mode that separates these novels from the rest of the canon, a difference that has yet to be fully defined.

F. O. Matthiessen attributes at least part of the difference to Melville's personal exhaustion,[1] but there are indications that perhaps Melville's departures from his previous work were deliberate and that the final effects were carefully planned. The fictional mode of the canon up to and including the early short stories is one which uses perspective to reveal character. The way in which an individual regards himself or his environment and his ability to recognize the limitations of single perspectives are important factors in his choice of actions and in the reader's study of those actions. Perspective thus functions as a structural device upon which Melville can ground his fiction and by means of which the reader is permitted to comprehend that fiction. As has been suggested, a study

1. *American Renaissance* (London, 1941), p. 491.

49

of the psychological perspectives of Tommo, Redburn, White Jacket, and Pierre facilitates not only our understanding of the characters themselves, but also and even more importantly our understanding of the total work in which each appears. When we turn to *Israel Potter* or *The Confidence-Man*, however, we discover that the fictional mode no longer uses perspective to reveal character. The reader is able to do nothing more than speculate about the central characters or the world which surrounds them. Melville seems to have deliberately changed the fictional mode so as to frustrate our complete understanding of action and character.

One of the first indications of a change in fictional mode occurs in "Benito Cereno." Although the psychological perspective of Delano serves to reveal *his* character, it provides an insufficient means for comprehending the fictional world of the story. A comparison of the function of Delano's perspective with, for example, that of the perspective of White Jacket reveals that the earlier story is constructed so that the reader may ultimately rely on the way White Jacket regards the world. As White Jacket realizes the limitations of his initial posture, he shifts his physical as well as his psychological position. Eventually the reader is able to accept White Jacket's perspective as reliable, still limited by human capabilities but not by individual blindness. But Delano is not White Jacket, and we certainly cannot comprehend the situation and events in "Benito Cereno" by relying on Delano's perspective, for here his view of the world remains as limited as does Pierre's. In *Pierre,* however, a further angle of vision is provided by the narrator, who interprets as well as presents, a method which makes Pierre one who is observed rather than identified with. This distance between narrator and central figure is accompanied by a general change of tone from the earlier books, for with the narrator moving from center stage to the wings, the central figure is viewed with an ironic detachment which contributes to the sense of isolation and futility that marks the book. What Melville provides, therefore, in both *White Jacket* and *Pierre* is not only a reliable narrator but more importantly a reasonably reliable perspective from which the story can be approached. In "Benito Cereno," however—also told by a third-person narrator—the narrative voice is so scrupulously objective and Delano's perspective, though it only controls the first part of the story, so clearly limited that the reader is unable to get to the heart of the events related. It is as though Melville is incorporating the limitations of perspective into the fiction itself. The final section of the narrative is given to trial testimony, a fictional device that emphasizes the limitations of individual perspectives, for we have the testimony of the witnesses but not the actuality which they talk about. In other words, the fictional mode of "Benito Cereno," unlike that of *White Jacket* and *Pierre*, is deliberately constructed so as to force the reader to remain at a distance. One can speculate about the events, but he is finally left with only brilliantly illuminated perspectives of those events.

Melville's first novel to be structured on the basis of this new mode is *Israel Potter*, a story of futility and isolation. A giant in chains, secret military plans that never seem to come to fruition, naval battles in which the victor sinks while the loser remains afloat, and a central figure whose basic talent is his ability to survive are characteristic of a book in which actions are determined less by an individual's plans than by circumstances. The possibility for achievement as a result of personal endeavor, a possibility which plays a major role in *Redburn* and *White Jacket*, is only secondarily important in *Israel Potter*. Man is here cut off from the universe, from his fellow beings, and perhaps even from himself. The influence of chance and environment on actions limits the possibility of individual choice. Events do not frustrate Israel's decisions; they determine them. Tommo, Redburn, and Pierre encounter the physical world after they have chosen to act; Israel encounters it prior to choice. *Israel Potter* is thus a story which should be and is constructed in such a way as to frustrate a reader's desire to comprehend fully what happens. Both thematically and artistically the term "psychological perspective" as it has previously been used in this study is not a part of *Israel Potter*. The action of the book negates any possibility of Israel's conceiving of himself as separate from his environment, as a distinct being with an identity of his own, and such a conception is necessary if one is to have a perspective of his world, for perspective is a term which implies distance from an object. An exile and an enemy, Potter can afford only an identity which is fluid, one constantly capable of change. Because of the world in which he lives, he is and must be a faceless hero. Since the central figure is never able to understand himself with regard to his world—implying that the relation between self and world is incomprehensible—it is artistically appropriate that the reader not be able to either. Perspective as a way of revealing character and a method for comprehending the action of a book is, therefore, fittingly and necessarily absent. The fictional mode of *Israel Potter* is, thus, not the sign of Melville's exhaustion but rather that of an artist seeking to reflect meaning in form.

The world of which Israel is a part is described physically in the book's opening chapter, "The Birthplace of Israel." The landscape is characterized by mountainous terrain, sterility, and solitude. "At the present day, some of those mountain townships present an aspect of singular abandonment. Though they have never known aught but peace and health, they . . . look like countries depopulated by plague and war."[2] The country is lovely but lonely during the summer almost as though it invites the presence of nature but not that of man. In autumn, even the birds leave, and drizzling mists settle upon mountains "left bleak and sere" (p. 5). When the snows come, all communication stops. "Such, at this day, is the country which gave birth to our hero" (p. 5). As he matures, Israel adjusts to this world and becomes caught up in a stream of continuous movement. When he goes to sea, for example, his journeys from Providence to Antigua, Puerto Rico, Africa, Nantucket, and the South Seas are mentioned in less than three paragraphs. The rapidity with which this movement is presented suggests a meaninglessness and loneliness which come to be characteristic of Potter's story as he moves quickly and aimlessly from place to place. Continually seen as one alone, betrayed, or used by those with whom he does establish relationships, Israel is forced to hunt, because his home is too rocky for farming and because predation is the most effective way to survive. The early action, unlike the scenic description, is narrated in an abrupt and hurried fashion which contrasts sharply with the smoothly flowing opening of *Pierre*. In both books, however, technique is appropriate to meaning. As a youth, Pierre glides through his daily life, but Israel is tossed from one situation to another. The opening chapters of *Pierre* are told in such a way as to emphasize the comfortable security of Pierre's home at Saddle Meadows, a home which he then rejects. No such sense of home is presented in *Israel Potter*, for the narrator wishes to establish Israel's world as one of lonely isolation, one which rejects *him*.

In such a world, it is evident that there is no pattern of events

2. *Israel Potter: His Fifty Years of Exile* (New York, 1963), p. 2. All subsequent references to *Israel Potter* will be to this edition and will appear in the text.

upon which Israel can depend, a fact indicated in a number of ways of which the abrupt linking of unlooked-for events is but one.

Three days out of Boston harbor, the brigantine was captured by the enemy's ship *Foy*, of twenty guns. Taken prisoner with the rest of the crew, Israel was afterwards put on board the frigate *Tartar*, with immediate sailing orders for England. Seventy-two were captives in this vessel. Headed by Israel, these men—halfway across the sea—formed a scheme to take the ship, but were betrayed by a renegade Englishman. As ring-leader, Israel was put in irons, and so remained till the frigate anchored at Portsmouth. There he was brought on deck; and would have met perhaps some terrible fate, had it not come out, during the examination, that the Englishman had been a deserter from the army of his native country ere proving a traitor to his adopted one (pp. 16–17).

In such a passage the emphasis is upon the outcome of an act, the change that constantly occurs, rather than upon the situations themselves. Many of the changes are shown to be the result of improbable circumstances as, for example, the fact of Israel being redeemed from some terrible fate because he was turned in by a traitor. There is little causal relationship between events, and this is reinforced by the narrator's tendency to shift back and forth between past and present. "And here in the black bowels of the ship, sunk low in the sunless sea, our poor Israel *lay* for a month, like Jonah in the belly of the whale. But one bright morning, Israel *is* hailed from the deck" (p. 17—emphasis mine). It is thus as difficult to find a pattern to the sequence of time as it is to the sequence of events. Israel has no home, no friend, no particular duty to perform other than to survive. He rushes from one narrow escape to another, seeking "with stubborn patience to habituate himself to misery, but still hold aloof from despondency" (p. 28). Hunted like an animal, he is often referred to as an animal, "harassed day and night, hunted from food and sleep, driven from hole to hole like a fox in the woods" (p. 36). The world is thus pictured as one in which events occur for no logical reason, in which time seems to be of little significance, and in which personal relationships are casual.

During the course of his adventures, Israel encounters three individuals who function as rather obvious foils to the faceless hero. Ben Franklin, John Paul Jones, and Ethan Allen have distinct personalities and act on definite assumptions fittingly summarized by Poor Richard's maxim that "God helps them that help themselves." In contrast to Potter, they are presented as having well-defined psychological perspectives; they conceive of themselves as separate from their environment, able to choose, act, and influence events. In reality, however, they have scarcely more opportunity to direct their own actions than does Israel. Paul Jones, of the three the one with whom Israel spends the most time, feels that in order to succeed he must have "a separate, supreme command; no leader and no counsellor but himself" (p. 74). In spite of this self-confidence, he is unable to conquer the elements, and his battles are frequently hindered or stopped by the power of the winds or the shape of the land: "The career of this stubborn adventurer signally illustrates the idea that since all human affairs are subject to organic disorder, since they are created in and sustained by a sort of half-disciplined chaos, hence he who in great things seeks success must never wait for smooth water, which never was and never will be, but, with what straggling method he can, dash with all his derangements at his object, leaving the rest to Fortune" (p. 151).

The meeting between Jones's *Bon Homme Richard* and the British *Serapis* is an illustration of the illusionary aspect of Jones's personal independence. As depicted by the narrator, the battle is not masterminded by Jones but arranged by invisible powers, conducted as "an intestine feud," and concluded without a winner. Chaos and death are the only results of this mutually destructive battle in which it is almost impossible to tell friend from foe, a fact which underscores the meaninglessness of psychological perspective. The outcome is determined less by human plan than by chance. When fire becomes the common foe of both ships, mutual obliteration seems inevitable. "The men of either knew hardly which to do—strive to destroy the enemy, or save themselves" (p. 170). When the *Serapis* strikes her colors, the *Richard* is the victor, but in name only: "About ten o'clock the *Richard*, gorged with slaughter, wallowed heavily, gave a long roll, and blasted by tornadoes of sulphur, slowly sunk, like Gomorrah, out of sight" (p. 173). This ironic sinking of the victorious *Richard* as well as the bestial qualities suggested by its death throes and the allusion to Gomorrah are indicative of the futility and sordidness of human actions. In spite of Paul Jones's conception of himself, the control of his destiny lies primarily with forces outside himself. Survival, not growth and achievement, must be his concern as well as Potter's.

Israel and Jones part company later when Jones's new ship, the *Ariel*, and an unidentified English ship meet and for an hour practice mutual deception as each tries to learn the identity of the other, an endeavor fitting for the sequel to follow. Confusion results, and Israel accidently finds himself aboard the English ship, which flees from and finally escapes the *Ariel*. Once again his plans are abruptly changed by an unlooked for set of circumstances; once again he is forced to save himself in a hostile environment. The fact that his task is made slightly easier by his speaking the same language and wearing the same clothes as his captors is actually a continuation of the theme of "intestine feud," for he must seek a place and an identity among people who are both his brothers and his enemies.

Israel's search, a striking example of Melville's ability to relate form to meaning, is a crystallization of the book itself, for the English ship is a microcosm of the hostile world in which the protagonist must find a place among his fellow men by relying totally on his wits. It is also an example of Melville's use of physical place to parallel thought. During the course of the chapter, Israel moves downward from the ship's maintop, as does White Jacket, in seeking a place with every group aboard. But Israel's experience is distinctly different from White Jacket's. In each case he is faced with the same question: " 'Who are you?' " Unable to answer satisfactorily, he is forced to shift his physical position and to continue trying to find a group with which he can identify. His movement carries him down to the hold of the ship, where, "as a last resort, he dived down among the *holders*" (p. 179), but there he is once again informed, " 'you don't belong.' " Even when he seeks a place among the waisters, "the vilest caste of an armed ship's company" (p. 179), he is rejected. At last, day breaks, and he is discovered. In frustration at not being able to identify Israel, who now pretends to be mad, the officer-of-the-deck has him led away by the master-at-arms. Asked by the captain to what end he leads Israel about, the master-at-arms replies, " 'To no end in the world, sir. I keep leading him about because he has no final destination' " (p. 186). Again Israel is asked who he is, and again he is unable to answer. "So they resumed their devious wanderings" (p. 188). Artistically, the entire chapter is a superb example of the author as craftsman visually illustrating his book's theme.

"Who are you?" is the major question in *Israel Potter*, one which indicates the difference between this book and those preceding it, for the earlier central figures all have a strong sense of personal identity, the result of a consciousness of place which enables them to view their world from a specific psychological perspective. Here, however, the form and theme of the book combine in such a way as to ensure that no one, neither character nor reader, can be certain of Israel's proper place within his environment. Potter is caught up in events and swept along. He has no consciousness of himself as someone distinct, someone who can influence the course of events. The London scenes which conclude the book emphasize this point. Whether buried in the clay pits of the brick yard or compared to a herring in the "gulf-stream of humanity" (p. 210), Israel is depicted as merely one other brick or one other fish. He has no distinctive identity and is in no way free to act independently. "Somehow he continued to subsist, as those tough old oaks of the cliffs, which, though hacked at by hailstones of tempests, and even wantonly maimed by the passing woodman, still, however cramped by rival trees and fettered by rocks, succeed, against all odds, in keeping the vital nerve of the tap-root alive" (p. 220). The structure of the book as well as individual scenes within it are shaped so as to emphasize a world in which man cannot hope to determine his own actions. Events force him to respond. The best he can do is to find a place and hold on.

What little the reader learns about the personal identity of Israel Potter is considerable when compared to what he learns about the central figure of Melville's final novel, *The Confidence-Man*. The disguises and mental agility which enable Potter to evade his pursuers are used by the confidence man to evade the reader as well as characters within the book. We do not even know what the confidence man looks like underneath his various disguises, let alone what he thinks. In no other work of the Melville canon is the personal identity of a character as much a mystery as it is here, and appropriately in no other work of the canon is perspective employed as it is here. Given all its implications, perspective was extremely useful to Melville throughout this 1846–1856 decade as a reflection of his thought. Now in *The Confidence-Man*, whether seen as an ultimate statement of blackness or as indirectly leading to something more hopeful, the subtleties of perspective are given their fullest treatment. In *Israel Potter* psychological perspective is significant by its absence; in *The Confidence-Man* it is a tool of the hero. No longer a device used by the author to reveal character, it is now a weapon to be used by the protagonist against his victims.[3] The ability to use perspective is what distinguishes the confidence man from all other Melvillean heroes. Of the various faces presented in the book, which, if any, is the confidence man's own we never know. What his own psychological perspective is we can only guess. We know only that he is a man who can use the psychological perspective of others to establish supremacy over them. He is so skillful that he seems frequently to manipulate his intended victims for fun as well as profit, engaging in the second half of the book in lengthy debates with fellow confidence men where there seems to be little chance of monetary reward. Perspective is thus basic to *The Confidence-Man* because it explains, first of all, the technique of the book's hero, who is cleverly attuned to the psychological perspectives of those around him.

More than this, however, the protagonist's ability to use perspective for his own ends is suggestive of what an author does in constructing a work of fiction. Both confidence man and author create and manipulate psychological perspectives in order to achieve predetermined effects. The importance of this implied similarity lies in the cynical suggestion that the words of an author can be trusted no more than those of the confidence man. Both are manipulators, and perhaps neither is reliable. It is in this novel, where he most thoroughly and despairingly explores the relationship between fiction and truth, that Melville most clearly reflects meaning in form. Perspective becomes a device used by both author and hero to deceive their victims, who, in the case of the author, are the readers. The fictional mode thus resembles the fiction itself, for the reader discovers that the author, like his hero, is using perspective not to reveal but to obscure.

The Confidence-Man, like *Mardi* and *Clarel*, is structured upon a series of dramatic confrontations between the protagonist and the world around him. As in no other work in the canon, however,

---

3. In a 1964 "Afterword" to the Signet edition of *The Confidence-Man*, R. W. B. Lewis makes the following comment: "The first and most accomplished of the confidence men in the novel is the author; and his first potential victim is the inattentive reader" (New York, 1964, p. 265). I hope Professor Lewis is suggesting that the second potential victim is the *attentive* reader, for we are drawn, as he says, "through intellectual laughter to something like intellectual panic" (p. 264). It is easy, by the book's end, to adopt a stance like Egbert, Mark Winsome's disciple. Lewis' comments point to an interpretation which supports what Melville is doing in the book with perspective.

here the significance of the confrontations is directed outward, away from the protagonist, rather than inward, toward him. While revealing little about the confidence man, the book indicates a great deal about the world, a fact which relates it more closely to *Israel Potter* than to any of Melville's other works. The first chapter contains an action symbolic of the form that the book is to take. After coming aboard the *Fidele* at sunrise on the first day of April, a date which should make the reader wary of what he is told even by an author, the confidence man moves through the crowd with a slate upon which he writes several definitions of charity, all of which are St. Paul's, not his. The way in which the definitions are written indicates the protagonist's future technique. "The word charity, as originally traced, remained throughout uneffaced, not unlike the left-hand numeral of a printed date, otherwise left for convenience in blank."[4] The words written on the right-hand portion of the slate are changed at will in order to provide different characteristics of "charity," an absolute which remains unchanged but never defined. Similarly, during the book the confidence man, maintaining a consistent allegiance to "charity," alters his appearance as well as his argument in order to extort money and confidence from his victims. The action is thus a series of confrontations between two psychological perspectives, at least one of which is always contrived. It is the task of the confidence man, in the guise which is most appropriate to the particular confrontation, to make the many minds referred to in the title of Chapter 2 view the world from a single psychological perspective.

Disguised as a crippled Negro, for example, the protagonist appears among the passengers early in order to set up later meetings. This disguise seems carefully chosen to elicit a response of distrust. Whether he is really crippled or even a Negro is a question raised by "a limping, gimlet-eyed, sour-faced person" (p. 11) whose single eye and leg are " 'emblematic of his one-sided view of humanity' " (p. 15). When several other passengers begin to doubt the Negro's authenticity, he is able to specify that there are men aboard who will vouch for him. These men, of course, are only the confidence man himself in various disguises. The scene is important, for the fact that the "ge'mmen" mentioned are now viewed by the pas-

4. *The Confidence-Man: His Masquerade* (New York, 1954), p. 3. All subsequent references to *The Confidence-Man* will be to this edition and will appear in the text.

sengers as people to be trusted, who in vouching for the authenticity of someone else will not have their own authenticity questioned. The role of the crippled Negro is not important for the money it earns but because it establishes the psychological perspective from which the young minister, the country merchant, and others will regard the later disguises.

Profit seems to be only one of the confidence man's motives, for he frequently initiates encounters which do not promise much if any material reward. He appears to be motivated at these times by the sheer enjoyment of the game, the pleasure of playing with perspective. His meeting with the Missouri bachelor, for example, offers greater challenge than reward. The bachelor's thoughts—" 'I have confidence in distrust' " (p. 123)—are just the opposite of those professed by the confidence man in his guise of an herb-doctor. Though the Missourian is aware of nature's healthy aspect, he is more impressed by its destructive side: " 'Look you, nature! I don't deny but your clover is sweet, and your dandelions don't roar; but whose hailstones smashed my windows?' " (p. 124). To the confidence man, this is a hard case, a challenge which is hurled directly at him. Wagging the raccoon tail of his cap in the herb-doctor's face, the bachelor taunts him, " 'Can you, the fox, catch him?' " (p. 126). The herb-doctor changes the subject, seemingly to permit the conversation to become more cordial but in reality to set up his next disguise. He has accepted the challenge and has gathered all the information necessary to dupe this misanthropic enthusiast. Reappearing as a representative of the Philosophical Intelligence Office, an employment agency, the confidence man takes the opportunity to suggest views on the subject of human nature different from those set forward by the Missourian: " 'Anew regard the man-child . . . in the perspective of his developments' " (p. 139). The Missourian accuses him of punning " 'with ideas as another man may with words' " (p. 141), but eventually he yields and even adopts the confidence man's argument. " 'Yes, yes, yes,' excitedly cried the bachelor, as the light of this new illustration broke in, 'yes, yes; and now that I think of it, how often I've sadly watched my Indian corn in May, wondering whether such sickly, half-eaten sprouts, could ever thrive up into the stiff, stately spear of August' " (p. 143). The confidence man finally convinces him at least to experiment with these "new views of boys, and men, too" (p. 145). As the bachelor later realizes, he was vulnerable on "the castle's south side, its genial one"

(p. 148). Because of limited psychological perspective, he is not prepared for an attack from all sides, a situation upon which the confidence man thrives. "Was the man a trickster, it must be more for the love than the lucre. Two or three dirty dollars the motive to so many nice wiles?" (p. 148). That the confidence man does indeed love the game is apparent in the fact that he approaches the Missourian in yet a third disguise. As the cosmopolitan, he argues from another angle but one which still insists on a single perspective. " 'If I take your parable right,' " says the bewildered Missourian, " 'the meaning is, that one cannot enjoy life with gusto unless he renounce the too-sober view of life' " (p. 153).

Like the actions of the protagonist, the book itself is structured so as to deceive, to force the victim to concentrate on appearances rather than on what, if anything, lies beneath the surface. Leon Seltzer feels that "Melville's novel is, in its very refusal to illuminate what is behind the appearances it presents, . . . able to increase our consciousness of the inscrutable nature of reality."[5] This statement is true, but it does not go far enough in indicating what Melville does. In *Israel Potter* he refuses to reveal what lies behind appearances, but in *The Confidence-Man* he questions the appearance itself. As Seltzer himself points out, "the obvious circumstance that all of Melville's book is fiction anyway (the author is so bold as to declare this outright in his three chapters on authorial commentary) finally reduces all . . . logical considerations to complete irrelevance."[6] Melville not only declares the fiction but also illustrates it by his style, which is as deceptive as that of the confidence man. Attempts to uncover the hero's true character are inevitably defeated: "This . . . added a third angle to the discussion, which now became a sort of triangular duel, and ended, at last, with but a triangular result" (p. 104). A similar result greets the reader who tries to decide whether some of Melville's sentences are very deep or merely very murky—"In vain did his counsel, striving to make out the derangement to be where, in fact, if anywhere, it was, urge that, to hold otherwise, to hold that such a being as Goneril was sane, this was constructively a libel upon womankind" (p. 68). Similarly, when one examines the chapters on the techniques of characterization, he discovers that Melville is playing with the whole

5. "Camus's Absurd and the World of Melville's *Confidence-Man*," *PMLA* 82 (March 1967):22.
6. Seltzer, p. 21.

concept of Truth. In Chapter 14 he calls for characters to be true to real life even in its inconsistencies but finds it strange in Chapter 33 "that in a work of amusement, this severe fidelity to real life should be exacted by any one" (p. 206). Both statements are well defended, and each is by itself convincing. Taken together, however, they offer contradictory views of the same object. Neither is any more reliable than one of the protagonist's disguises. The reader, who must take everything on a faith born of confidence in the author, finds that confidence cleverly and continually undermined by sentences and statements such as those above. Both author and hero manipulate perspective so that there is finally no difference between fiction and truth, between story and fictional mode. The work of fiction and the words of the confidence man are both artful disguises designed to victimize the innocent, and both are symbolized in Chapter 44 by the revolving Drummond Light, which rays "away from itself all around it" (p. 271). Both story and fictional mode direct attention outwards to the words that have been spoken, rather than inwards to whatever meaning they conceal.

The close relationship between fiction and mode may be clearly seen in the chapters with Charlie Noble, Mark Winsome, and Egbert. Though the confidence man asks both Charlie and Egbert for money, his central interest would seem to be in the pleasure of debate. Unlike the first half of the book, which presents a series of confrontations between seducer and seduced, the second half involves debates between confidence men of equal ability. Each man, much like an author, hides his true identity and discusses or argues questions, "scholastically and artistically" (p. 213), from psychological perspectives which are deliberately formulated for the issue of the moment. The conversation between Egbert and the confidence man as well as the subject of that conversation illustrates how one can avoid revealing his own thoughts by playing with psychological perspective. When Egbert asks how the confidence man likes Mark Winsome, for example, the reply avoids a direct answer: "'That each member of the human guild is worthy respect, my friend,' rejoined the cosmopolitan, 'is a fact which no admirer of that guild will question; but that, in view of higher natures, the word sublime, so frequently applied to them, can, without confusion, be also applied to man, is a point which man will decide for himself; though, indeed, if he decide it in the affirmative, it is not for me to object'" (pp. 225–26). Their discussion centers upon a hypothetical situation involving two hypothetical friends: "'Mind, now, you must work up your imagination, and, as much as possible, talk and behave just as if the case supposed were a fact'" (p. 226). Not only is this in reality what an author does in creating a work of fiction, but it is also what Melville seems to be saying explicitly in the three chapters on characterization. He looks at the same subject from several angles, making each as convincing as possible but without committing himself to any.

This scene between Egbert and the cosmopolitan, when compared to the earlier ones in *Typee* or *Redburn*, is indicative of the central difference between *The Confidence-Man* and Melville's previous work. Here two individuals argue from psychological perspectives not their own about an issue in which they are not involved. Neither is vitally concerned about the outcome since the argument is hypothetical to begin with. The psychological perspectives of Tommo and Redburn, on the other hand, are not hypothetical. Each acts according to the way he personally views the world. His identity is revealed by a study of his perspective, which is thus an element of character rather than of plot. The form, as well as the meaning of the fiction, leads the reader inward by way of specific angles of vision toward the heart of a character; at the same time, it implies that man, who must necessarily regard objects from single perspectives, will never be able to comprehend what lies at the center. In *The Confidence-Man*, however, Melville no longer cherishes "expectations with regard to some mode of infallibly discovering the heart of man" (p. 79). Perspective no longer reveals character; it now furthers the plot, directing the reader outward away from the heart of man. The fictional mode of the book does the same thing by its deceptive phrasing and its fluid handling of subject. At the end the reader can trust neither the author nor the protagonist. In the earlier works if man is prevented by human limitations from ever striking through the mask that hid Truth, in *The Confidence-Man* he is forced to question the very existence of Truth itself.

7

Conclusion–*Billy Budd, Sailor*

M

Y CONCERN in the preceding discussion of Melville's prose fiction is with the author's interest in perspective, both physical and psychological. I have sought not to prove a specific generalization about the use of perspective but to indicate that it functions importantly throughout the canon. The implications of the fact that man operates under the limitations of single perspectives influence the themes explored by Melville as well as the forms in which the explorations occur. Rather than restate these points, I would prefer to suggest in this concluding chapter that the critical disagreement concerning Melville's attitude toward Captain Vere in *Billy Budd, Sailor* can perhaps be illuminated by an analysis of psychological perspective as it operates within that story.

After the passing of more than three decades between the publication of *The Confidence-Man* and the writing of *Billy Budd*, Melville returned to the earlier fictional mode of *White Jacket* and *Moby-Dick* rather than to that discussed in Chapter 6 of this study.[1] Perspective again becomes a method whereby the author can reveal rather than obscure, and thus is an element of character rather than plot. However, in *Billy Budd* perspective is essentially thematic rather than artistic. It is the thesis of this study that Melville uses perspective to structure his novels so that form ultimately parallels content, as it does in the fall of White Jacket and the increasing isolation of Pierre. Such formal expressions of theme, however, do not operate significantly in Melville's last prose work. But perspective functions, as it does earlier, to reveal character and is thus

1. Dryden's "Epilogue" chapter in *Melville's Thematics of Form* works along similar lines as my discussion here of *Billy Budd*. My concern with perspective supports many of the conclusions he draws in that chapter with regard to the form of *Billy Budd*.

an aspect of the story which we should consider before assessing its final meaning. In choosing to act absolutely on the basis of a particular angle of vision, Vere condemns himself to the limitations of a single perspective. The narrative concerns itself with these limitations and in so doing suggests that instead of occupying a special role in the canon, Vere is very much like other Melvillean heroes who choose to act absolutely and who seek to deny personal responsibility for that choice.

The critical position which sees Vere as hero is well argued in Milton Stern's *The Fine Hammered Steel*: "Vere rejects both lure and quester. His heartbroken rejection of Budd as a beautiful impossibility in favor of an ugly reality, his decision to force his position of command to operate according to what his head dictates and his heart detests, is his acceptance of this world as the only possible one. It is not, as many critics have attempted to demonstrate, an acceptance of God and a submission to Fate. It is quite the opposite. It is Melville's reluctant, modified, but final acceptance of historical necessity in a naturalistic universe. It is a consequent call for man to control his fate by controlling his actions in the historical world —and it is also Melville's statement of inability to find the way to do so."[2] Stern's analysis—which describes Vere's action in the glowing terms appropriate to one who feels that Vere is Melville's "one real hero"—is significant both for what it says that Vere does and for what it says that Melville does. Vere and Melville are somehow identified so that Vere's story is also Melville's "acceptance of historical necessity." W. E. Sedgwick is even more explicit in stating that "it is not that Captain Vere (or Melville) has capitulated in the sense of abdicating his speculative mind and his idealism";[3] it is that he accepts the "sorrowful mystery of life," "the yoke of necessity." Therefore, according to Sedgwick, Melville reverses himself from his earlier writings, so that what "had been vanity before, to build a Chinese Wall in one's soul, is now the part of wisdom." Both Sedgwick and Stern read *Billy Budd* as Melville's answer to the dilemmas of human existence. Whether we call it an acceptance of God or an acceptance of necessity, the emphasis remains on the fact that it is Melville's acceptance. But the writings prior to *Billy Budd* stress the fact that in the Melvillean universe no absolute an-

2. Stern, p. 27.
3. *Herman Melville: The Tragedy of Mind* (Cambridge, Mass., 1945), p. 239.

swer is possible. Man is too limited to see all sides of an issue. The experience of the canon, therefore, seems to indicate that Vere's actions, like Ahab's, have personal rather than heroic implications.[4]

Vere does not become central until rather late in the story, but by then the narrator has emphasized the importance of perspective. It is, first of all, "an inside narrative,"[5] one which views the events as would an insider, someone privy to what actually happens though not necessarily to why it happens. The phrase has several implications, one of which is that other narratives of the same events are also possible. The word "inside" suggests that there are outside narratives, a suggestion supported by the story's inclusion of a newspaper account of the incidents. Even the use of the indefinite article hints of other inside narratives. One other implication of the phrase is that from his point of view what the narrator is about to relate is reliable, and, in comparison with the concluding official account, it probably is. After reading "Benito Cereno," *Israel Potter*, and *The Confidence-Man*, however, one cannot help wondering whether the events recounted in "an inside narrative" might not be interpreted in several ways.

Psychological perspective is further emphasized in the early sections of the story by the fact that the narrator stresses not events but individual responses to events as, for example, the contrasting responses of Lieutenant Ratcliffe and Captain Graveling to the impressment of Billy. The acquiescence of Billy himself is also emphasized, because it is indicative of the psychological perspective which underlies it, one which is later symbolized by Billy's physical perspective aboard the *Bellipotent*: "Life in the foretop well agreed with Billy Budd. There, when not actually engaged on the yards yet higher aloft, the topmen, who as such has been picked out for youth and activity, constituted an aerial club lounging at ease against the smaller stun'sails rolled up into cushions, spinning yarns like the lazy gods, and frequently amused with what was going on in the busy world of the decks below. No wonder then that a young fellow of Billy's disposition was well content in such society" (p.

---

4. An argument against seeing Vere as hero is persuasively presented by Charles Mitchell in "Melville and the Spurious Truth of Legalism," *Centennial Review of Arts and Science* 12 (1968):110–26. Mitchell also seeks to place *Billy Budd* in the larger context of the Melville canon.

5. *Billy Budd, Sailor,* ed. Harrison Hayford and Merton M. Sealts, Jr. (Chicago and London, 1962), p. 41. All subsequent references to *Billy Budd* will be to this edition and will appear in the text.

68). Such a physical location is appropriate to Billy, who psychologically is above the everyday world. He has no intuitive knowledge of evil and is, therefore, totally limited to a single perspective —a sharp contrast to Jack Chase, his counterpart in *White Jacket*, who is aware of other perspectives.

Billy's encounter with Claggart, the master-at-arms, centers upon the disparity between their perspectives. As the ship's chief of police, Claggart is "charged among other matters with the duty of preserving order on the populous lower gun decks" (p. 64), and thus his physical perspective is different from and as one-sided as Billy's. So also is his psychological perspective. Billy views the world from a postion of trust, one which admits no sense of evil; Claggart views it from a position of distrust. "For the adequate comprehending of Claggart by a normal nature these hints are insufficient. To pass from a normal nature to him one must cross 'the deadly space between'" (p. 74). Claggart's total sense of evil is juxtaposed to Billy's total sense of good. The confrontation is thus one between two equally limited psychological perspectives, one limited by innocence, the other by monomania. Given such a confrontation, "something decisive must come of it" (p. 90).

Unlike Claggart, Billy is completely unable to understand his enemy even when warned by an old Dansker who, from a psychological perspective based upon worldly experience, rightly assesses Claggart's actions. Claggart, however, is intellectually able to appreciate the significance of a different perspective. "One person excepted, [he] was perhaps the only man in the ship intellectually capable of adequately appreciating the moral phenomenon presented in Billy Budd" (p. 78). Claggart does not act out of misunderstanding. He knows what he is doing in seeking to destroy Billy just as Ahab does in his hunt for the white whale. When such men surrender to the evil within them, their natures recoil upon themselves. Had Billy "been conscious of having done or said anything to provoke the ill will of the official" (p. 88), he would have acted differently. But Claggart is conscious of the situation, and it is thus fitting that his action should lead to his own destruction.

"One person excepted," Claggart was the only man capable of appreciating Billy Budd. That brief phrase, which clearly refers to Captain Vere, hints of a similarity between the captain and the master-at-arms. Both men are capable of appreciating the significance of perspectives other than their own, but it is largely an intellectual appreciation. Each chooses to follow a course of action based upon a singularly limited psychological perspective, limited both by human capabilities and individual blindness. Though the following passage refers explicitly to Claggart, it hints further at the intellectual similarity of Claggart and Vere.

> But the thing which in eminent instances signalizes so exceptional a nature is this: Though the man's even temper and discreet bearing would seem to intimate a mind peculiarly subject to the law of reason, not the less in heart he would seem to riot in complete exemption from that law, having apparently little to do with reason further than to employ it as an ambidexter implement for effecting the irrational. That is to say: Toward the accomplishment of an aim which in wantonness of atrocity would seem to partake of the insane, he will direct a cool judgment sagacious and sound. These men are madmen, and of the most dangerous sort, for their lunacy is not continuous, but occasional, evoked by some special object; it is protectively secretive, which is as much as to say it is self-contained, so that when, moreover, most active it is to the average mind not distinguishable from sanity, and for the reason above suggested: that whatever its aims may be—and the aim is never declared—the method and the outward proceeding are always perfectly rational (p. 76).

"Even temper and discreet bearing," "a mind peculiarly subject to the law of reason," "a cool judgment sagacious and sound," these are qualities which also characterize Captain Vere. The accusation that he, too, employs reason "as an ambidexter implement for effecting . . . some special object" is never made, but in this and later passages the narrator invites speculation. The use of reason to effect the irrational is the act which best characterizes a nature such as Claggart's, a nature which knows of alternatives but which willfully limits itself to a single angle of vision and a destructive course of action. Certainly it is too severe to equate Claggart and Vere—Vere, for example, appreciates Billy emotionally as well as intellectually—but the similarities exist and should be considered before deciding that Vere is Melville's "one real hero." Vere responds to a set of circumstances which force him to act. The reader must be concerned with that act and the psychological perspective upon which it is based. Unlike other characters in the story, Vere has the ability and power to recognize and act upon perspectives different from his own. That possibility is rare in Melville and one which, if exercised, could indeed make Vere heroic.

Though Captain Vere does not appear until the second half of *Billy Budd*, he is introduced by the narrator earlier in discussing the events occurring at the time of Billy's impressment. The date of the story, the summer of 1797, is important to what happens later since it is only a few months after the Great Mutiny, an event "analogous to the distempering irruption of contagious fever in a frame constitutionally sound" (p. 55). Restoring and maintaining a healthy, and therefore ordered, navy is essential. Strong leaders are severely challenged, weak ones can easily break. The narrator mentions the names of several leaders in discussing these background events, men who command in different ways and inspire by different passions. The charismatic leader, like Admiral Nelson, seeks not "to terrorize the crew into base subjection, but to win them, by force of his mere presence and heroic personality, back to an allegiance if not as enthusiastic as his own yet as true" (p. 59). Captain Vere, on the other hand, is a leader "mindful of the welfare of his men, but never tolerating an infraction of discipline" (p. 60).[6] A disciplinarian in the summer of 1797, fully aware of the events occurring a short while before and commanding a ship whose crew, like others in the British Navy, is partially composed of criminals and impressed men, would probably react to a threatened mutiny in a way very different from Admiral Nelson's. Even if one does not wish to conclude from the presentation of each man's characteristics that Vere is the lesser of the two men, he should notice that, no matter how necessary Vere's later actions may seem, the narrator in the early pages indicates that other men might respond differently. When the story focuses on Vere, it is as a specific individual rather than as a representative hero.

From Captain Vere's perspective, one that reflects both his temperament and the current naval crisis, there can be only one response to Billy Budd's killing of Claggart: " 'Struck dead by an angel of God. Yet the angel must hang!' " (p. 101). It is a response like that of Pierre when he decides to leave Saddle Meadows, for both men react absolutely to situations where alternative possibilities

6. For a recent comparison of these two versions of the naval commander, see Ralph W. Willett, "Nelson and Vere: Hero and Victim in *Billy Budd, Sailor*," *PMLA* 82 (October 1967):370–76.

might be available; their subsequent actions are entirely the result of the choice. Pierre's decision is based on a limited psychological perspective, and Vere's is equally so. Pierre chooses to follow the heart, Vere the head: "The father in him . . . was replaced by the military disciplinarian" (p. 100).

The fact that Vere's is only one of several possible decisions is emphasized by the reaction of the ship's surgeon, who, having been informed by Vere that he plans to call a drumhead court, is "full of disquietude and misgiving" (p. 101). He not only has a different response but is also the first to suggest that what Vere is planning to do is not the usual course of action. Nor are the surgeon's thoughts restricted to himself, for the lieutenants and captain of marines "fully shared his own surprise and concern. Like him too, they seemed to think that such a matter should be referred to the admiral" (p. 102). Regardless of who is right, it is clear that the narrator wishes us to see that Vere speaks only for himself. "Whether Captain Vere, as the surgeon professionally and privately surmised, was really the sudden victim of any degree of aberration, every one must determine for himself by such light as this narrative may afford" (p. 102). Vere's actions are both personal and unusual. Whether they are necessary to preserve order or are the reflection of the thoughts of a weak and frightened man is crucial to determining if Vere is really Melville's "one real hero."

Being "a man of rapid decision" (p. 103) and fearing that mutiny might result from public announcement of the crime, Vere acts quickly: "Very far was he from embracing opportunities for monopolizing to himself the perils of moral responsibility, none at least that could properly be referred to an official superior or shared with him by his official equals or even subordinates. So thinking, he was glad it would not be at variance with usage to turn the matter over to a summary court of his own officers" (p. 104). But Vere is always very much in charge of the trial. He calls it, selects the judges, is the only witness, and dictates the verdict. When one judge, the officer of marines, concerns himself with motives rather than facts and directs some questions toward Billy, Vere interrupts after a glance from Billy, who deems Vere his friend: "'It seems to me, the point you make is hardly material. Quite aside from any conceivable motive actuating the master-at-arms, and irrespective of the provocation to the blow, a martial court must needs in the present case confine its attention to the blow's consequence, which consequence justly is to be deemed not otherwise than as the striker's deed' " (p. 107). As the narrator is quick to point out, this speech indicates a prejudgment, one that is immediately impressed upon each of the three officers. Vere continues to shut off debate both by his words and by "a glance more effective than words" (p. 108) at the first lieutenant.

After Billy leaves the cabin, the three judges begin deliberation upon a verdict, but once again it is Vere who directs the court though he would prefer to think differently: " 'Hitherto I have been but the witness, little more' " (p. 109). In his words, which, according to the narrator, are suggestive "of a certain pedantry" imputed to Vere by other naval captains, Vere makes himself most vulnerable to the charge that he uses "a cool judgment sagacious and sound" to accomplish an aim which is never declared. He sympathizes with the court's hesitancy, the product of the conflict between duty and " 'scruple vitalized by compassion,' " but insists that its concern must be with duty. Scruples enervate decision. " 'Do these buttons that we wear attest that our allegiance is to Nature?' " (p. 110). No longer free agents, they are not responsible for the rigor of the law. " 'Let not warm hearts betray heads that should be cool' " (p. 111). Personal feelings must be ruled out. By the Articles of War, Billy has committed a capital crime which may be acquitted in heaven, but not on earth. " 'War looks but to the frontage, the appearance' " (p. 112). The law and not the officers are responsible. Since attack may come at any moment either from the enemy or the sailors, it is necessary that a decision be reached immediately. "Tacitly leaving the three" to decide, Vere then crosses to the other side of the room. "Loyal lieges, plain and practical, though at bottom they dissented from some points Captain Vere had put to them, they were without the faculty, hardly had the inclination, to gainsay one whom they felt to be an earnest man, one too not less their superior in mind than in naval rank" (p. 113). The trial serves merely to rubberstamp Vere's earlier decision.

The major points of Vere's argument, one well stated and quite persuasive, recall similar words by Ahab, Pierre, and Plinlimmon. In "The Symphony" chapter of *Moby-Dick*, Ahab also rejects compassion and personal responsibility, arguing that as the agent of powers greater than he, he must continue his hunt. But man cannot abdicate responsibility by attributing it to the Fates, the Articles of War, or the buttons on his chest. One of Melville's major concerns in *White Jacket* is to attack this very concept, and the discussion of the Articles of War in that book is particularly interesting when read alongside Vere's argument. In addition, Vere's emphasis on the opposition of the interests of this world to those of the next recalls Plotinus Plinlimmon's pamphlet on chronometricals and horologicals and its argument in favor of a capitulation to the demands of this world. With such similarities between the thoughts of Vere and those of earlier figures, the reader's response to the action of the captain of the *Bellipotent* can only be one of two. Either (as Sedgwick has stated and Stern suggested) Melville completely reverses himself as the result of his realization of necessity and the impossibility of his earlier ideals, or he is presenting in Vere a character who, in his decision to act absolutely, is strikingly similar to the figures of his earlier works. Vere chooses a course of action which is equally absolute and equally the result of a single perspective. It is, therefore, one which is equally open to criticism. Vere's action is not necessarily the best choice but merely one possible choice. "Says a writer whom few know, 'Forty years after a battle it is easy for a noncombatant to reason about how it ought to have been fought. It is another thing personally and under fire to have to direct the fighting while involved in the obscuring smoke of it'" (p. 114). Such a passage surely expresses sympathy for Vere's situation, but it in no way endorses the wisdom or justice of the captain's action. If, however, characters in other parts of the canon err by choosing to act absolutely on the basis of their own limited perspectives, then the same point should be considered in assessing Vere's decision. The narrator understands Vere, but he makes no attempt to support the captain's action.

Ninety minutes after being confronted by Claggart, Billy is told that he is to be executed. In emphasizing the brevity of this time span, the narrator invites the thought that perhaps Vere's action is as spontaneous and precipitous as Billy's. Had he taken more time to consider, Vere might have acted differently. The fact that in Billy's final hours it is his innocence that is stressed suggests that the reader should question not only the necessity, but also the morality of Vere's choice. Vere's stated concern is for the *Bellipotent*, a position that is argued clearly, though in different terms, by Plotinus Plinlimmon. The similarity between Vere and Plinlimmon is discussed by Sedgwick in support of his contention that Melville has changed his attitude in his final book, accepting the path of virtuous expediency. "Now he [Melville] sees that because a man acts under a worldly necessity he does not therefore debase his humanity; his soul, be it immortal or not, is not soiled thereby."[7] But such a pragmatic approach to living is reflected in the actions of the chaplain, who does not attempt to save Billy from being made "a martyr to martial discipline" (p. 121). To do so would have been both idle and audacious since his actions also are dictated by law. Like Plinlimmon's ideal, he is Christ's servant serving institutions. "Why, then, is he there? Because . . . he lends the sanction of the religion of the meek to that which practically is the abrogation of everything but brute Force" (p. 122). This brief condemnation of religious expediency is precisely the same as that made in *White Jacket* and is extremely important for our understanding of Vere, since it follows immediately after Vere's support of the Articles of War. If the chaplain is vulnerable to this kind of criticism, how is it that Vere's soul is not soiled by his action? Both men serve the Articles of War. Has Melville changed so much that he now supports secular authority while continuing to criticize religious authority? It is more likely that just as the "Bosom Friend" chapter of *Moby-Dick* offers an indirect comment on Father Mapple's sermon so does the criticism of the chaplain of the *Bellipotent* imply the narrator's attitude toward Vere's speech before the drumhead court.

The few pages of the story which follow Billy's death are, as is frequently the case in Melville, more digressive in appearance than in reality, for they continue to stress the significance of perspective. To the account of the incidents already presented are added the report of a naval newspaper, which feels that "from the naval point of view" (p. 131) Vere's handling of the situation was correct, and a ballad of the sailors which presents Billy as a martyr to tyranny. The narrator's perspective, however, is such that he sees the partial validity expressed by both the newspaper and the ballad. These pages, therefore, suggest that we have been shown how the same event may be interpreted in a variety of ways when viewed by different observers. Three final hints about Vere and his motives further support this thesis. In describing the actions of the sailors at Billy's hanging, the narrator comments that "true martial discipline long continued superinduces in average man a sort of impulse whose operation at the official word of command much resembles in its

7. Page 240.

promptitude the effect of an instinct" (p. 127). Vere certainly is a man of martial discipline. Perhaps the promptitude of his decision is more instinctive than, as Stern suggests, the "sacrifice of self to the necessities of moral responsibility historically defined."[8] Or, like Claggart's undisclosed special objective in seeking to destroy Billy, perhaps Vere is motivated by ambition and a concern for how his career might be influenced by scandal or mutiny. Looking ahead to Vere's death, the narrator remarks that "the spirit that 'spite its philosophic austerity may yet have indulged in the most secret of all passions, ambition, never attained to the fulness of fame" (p. 129). Finally, the naval account of the affair praises Claggart's patriotism in carrying out his duties and offers him as a refutation of Samuel Johnson's assertion that "patriotism is the last refuge of a scoundrel" (p. 130). Vere also appeals to patriotism in speaking before the drumhead court. From the narrator's point of view, the naval assessment of Claggart's character is grossly inaccurate; surely Claggart is not a refutation of Johnson's view, which, therefore, is perhaps correct. Though these hints do not reveal what actually motivates Vere, they are sufficient to make one hesitate to accept the captain as Melville's "one real hero." Melville has not reversed himself. He continues to paint the portrait of men who choose to act absolutely—and, therefore, destructively—on the basis of a single and necessarily limited angle of vision.

Perspective, as it is used in the Melville canon, functions both thematically and artistically. Throughout his writings, Melville explores the implications of the fact that given man's limitations, he can never realize his desire to comprehend an absolute. Greatness exists in the desire; tragedy in the limitations; wisdom in the realization of those limitations. Man is so created that he can never examine an object from more than one angle of vision at any given moment. Such characters as Redburn, White Jacket, and the confidence man come to understand the importance of this fact and learn to act accordingly. Others, like Pierre and Amasa Delano, do not and thus blindly continue to pursue a single course of action. Though Ahab and Vere fully appreciate the fact of perspective, they choose to blind themselves to its meaning. Such distinctions between characters suggest that in his writings Melville explores a

8. Stern, p. 27.

variety of possible influences of perspective on the individual. The significance of perspective fascinated Melville throughout his work, for it is the one fact of human existence that continues to frustrate man's desire for knowledge, a desire without which he can never be great.

But the thematic function of perspective in the canon has long been a matter of critical concern. This study suggests that Herman Melville is much more than thinker. He is an artist, a man conscious of the elements of his craft and able to use them to reflect thought in form. I have tried to show that the limitations imposed upon man's aspirations by his humanity are reflected in the patterning of events, the use of setting and imagery, and the choice of character. Melville's angles of vision, his use of perspective, are central to his novels, and an understanding of them is essential to our appreciation of the author as artist. Perspective, since it has both psychological implications and physical representations, provided Melville with a basic concept upon which he could build his art; it provides the reader with an approach to the heart of that fiction.

UNIVERSITY OF FLORIDA MONOGRAPHS

Humanities